The 21 Most Amazing Truths about Heaven

Dave Earley

BARBOUR
PUBLISHING

Published by Barbour Publishing, Inc., P.O. Box 719, Uhrichsville, Ohio 44683
www.barbourbooks.com

*Our mission is to publish and distribute inspirational products offering exceptional
value and biblical encouragement to the masses.*

 Member of the
Evangelical Christian
Publishers Association

Printed in the United States of America.
5 4 3 2 1

DEDICATION

In loving memory of
Bert and Bob Earley, and Carl Smith.
Your presence in Heaven makes me long to join you there.

ACKNOWLEDGMENTS

Many thanks to the team of people who made this project a reality.

- Cathy, for twenty-five wonderful years of very happy marriage. You make Earth more heavenly for me.
- Daniel, Andrew, and Luke. I am very proud of you guys.
- "Szechwan Chicken." You "proofread pretty."
- Rod Bradley and the Mighty Men, for your prayers.
- Paul Muckley, for contacting me about this book, and Tim Martins, president of Barbour Publishing, for suggesting the idea. May our great adventure continue.
- Kelly Williams, for managing the in-house process, and Yolanda Chumney, for handling the typesetting.
- Elmer Towns, for your great example and sponsorship.
- Norm Rohrer, for your helpful advice.
- Carol Ann, you are my favorite sister.
- Steve, you are my favorite brother.
- Sandy, you are such a blessing to us.

CONTENTS

Introduction

I am embarrassed to admit this, but for a long time I did not think much about Heaven. To be honest, I wasn't all that interested in Heaven. I had plenty to do and experience down here on Earth. Besides, what I knew about Heaven made it sound distant, overly vague, and frankly too boring to hold my interest.

Yet over the last few years that has all begun to change. Let me explain.

On January 12, 2002, after an exhausting war with illness, my mom went into the emergency room. We all knew she would never leave. Two days later, after silently saying good-bye to her family, she quietly slipped into eternity. Her departure planted a seed of curiosity in my heart about Heaven. I found myself daydreaming about what might be going on in Heaven.

> *I wonder what Mom is doing right now?*
> *I wonder what she looks like in Heaven?*
> *Is she singing and dancing?*
> *Is heaven as beautiful as they say?*
> *Can she see me right now?*
> *Does she miss me as much as I miss her?*

Three years later, Dad was worn out after a long battle with cancer. As one who was gifted at living and making the most of the here and now, he began to ask me questions about Heaven. He was lonesome for Mom, tired of pain, and wanted to see Jesus. He said he wanted to go home. On the night of January 6, 2005, he got his wish—and crossed over into eternity.

For the next few weeks, as I'd watch the winter sun setting in its magnificent display of gold, tracing the edges of pink and purple clouds, I seriously pondered what life was like beyond those clouds. Heaven crowded its way into more and more of my thoughts. Questions kept popping up:

7

How "old" will Mom and Dad be in Heaven?
Will they live together as a married couple?
What do they eat and drink?
What work will Dad be doing?
What are they doing for fun?

I knew the Bible had much to say about Heaven, but I had never taken the time to thoroughly study it. I told myself, "Someday I'll do a detailed study of Heaven."

Exactly a year after my dad went to Heaven, my friend and editor, Paul Muckley, asked me to consider writing a book about Heaven. I jumped at the chance. What a perfect excuse to get my questions about Heaven answered.

In researching the subject, I was pleasantly surprised to discover that the Bible contains 582 references to Heaven in 550 verses. I learned that the Bible teaches amazingly big truths about Heaven. You might say it is the Garden of Eden, home, the Magic Kingdom, and Fantasy Island all combined and improved. I discovered that Heaven is anything but boring, and so much more.

I found that the first Christians had a rich preoccupation with Heaven based on the clear teachings of the Bible. Having a healthy, holy obsession with Heaven gave them hope and encouragement to face fierce trials and painful persecution. It provided resilient joy and supernatural strength. Studying the amazing truths about Heaven did the same for me. It also impacted my priorities down here in the present.

I believe that reading this book and gaining a better grasp of Heaven will not only satisfy your curiosity, but will undoubtedly give you authentic comfort, resounding peace, and tenacious energy as well. Plus, it will help prepare you to fully experience and enjoy your final forwarding address. . .Heaven.

Suggestions for getting the most out of this book:

1. Study each chapter with a sanctified imagination and a prayerful heart.

2. Share what you are learning with someone else. Better yet, study this book with a friend or a small group.

3. Reread chapters as they apply to the needs of your life.

4. Start living for eternity now so you will be prepared to enjoy and experience all of Heaven when you get there.

DON'T CUT YOUR FEET!

One of my all-time favorite books is *The Great Divorce* by C. S. Lewis. This novella was Lewis's version of *The Divine Comedy*. In Lewis's story, a busload of people from Hell are driven to the outskirts of Heaven and given the opportunity to stay there, if they so chose. Sadly, all but one prefer to return to the dirty, congested, urban fog of Hell rather than live in the brilliant morning light of Heaven.

I love Lewis's imagery of Hell as mere shadow compared to the firm substance of Heaven. He vividly portrays the people from Hell as shadows, ghosts, and man-shaped stains unfit for the crystal clear reality of Heaven.

There is a scene in the book I cannot erase from my mind. The phantoms from Hell have just arrived in the golden light shining on the lush beauty of the perpetual morning of Heaven. Gingerly, they step off the bus only to find that the reality of Heaven is so intense it literally hurts their feet. Lewis writes,

> *It was the light, the grass, the trees, that were*
> *different; made of some different substance, so*
> *much solider than things in our country, that men*
> *were ghosts by comparison*
> *. . . .Reality is harsh to the feet of shadows.*[1]

"Reality is harsh to the feet of shadows." Make no mistake.

Heaven exists. It is more real than anywhere you have ever been. In fact, Earth is mere shadow compared to the dense substance of Heaven. Heaven is reality. It is so real that it would cut the feet of the unprepared.

Wired for Eternity

As a pastor, I have had the privilege and responsibility of officiating at numerous funerals. There is always something awkward, foreign, unwanted, and extremely painful about the death of someone we love. Even if the person was very old and ill, the cold reality of death never fails to knock the wind out of those left behind. This is because we innately sense that we were made for something more than a casket.

Author Randy Alcorn notes that, worldwide, 3 people die every second, 180 every minute, almost 11,000 per hour, and over 250,000 every day[2]. Yet death still stuns us. It just doesn't seem right. Why? We have an instinctive awareness that we are destined for life beyond the grave.

This nagging sense that we are to live forever *somewhere* is the universal dream of mankind. It is so integrated into the human psyche that nearly every religion has been built upon its expectation. While opinions, philosophies, and religions may differ, few people accept death as the end of life. Elaborate rituals and quaint customs permeate the cultures of all peoples from all time. From the native warriors of the American plains, to the primitive tribesmen of the jungles, to the sophisticated mystics of the East, virtually every tradition has some system of belief regarding the afterlife. Every current poll shows that an overwhelming majority of Americans believe in life after death. Why? Our Creator has endowed each of us with an inherent knowledge of an afterlife.

Wise King Solomon told us why we have a built-in hunger

for Heaven when he spoke of God having "set eternity in the hearts of men" (Ecclesiastes 3:11). It only makes sense that if God placed this desire for eternity in our hearts, then it must be real. It is also logical that if eternity is real, God would give us some indication of what it will be like. So it should come as no surprise that He did. In 582 references in 550 verses, the Bible gives dozens of amazing truths about the eternal home of believers. This book will explore twenty-one of the major realities of Heaven.

One of the amazing truths about Heaven is that it is more than a wish, an analogy, a state of mind, or an ethereal realm. Heaven is an intensely real, acutely authentic, undeniably factual, literal place.

Heaven is a literal place, more real than anywhere you have ever been.

One major reason I struggled to get overly excited about Heaven was that I had a hard time finding comfort in the notion of being a disembodied spirit, dwelling in a vague state of nonphysical existence, somehow hovering in a mystical, ethereal realm totally unlike anything I had ever seen, known, or imagined. Thinking of Heaven as a really swell state of mind simply could not sustain my attention.

Fortunately, the more I studied the Bible on the subject of Heaven, the more it became obvious that Heaven is a real place, every bit as tangible, actual, literal, and concrete as the chair you are sitting in today. Granted, it is a much, much better, higher, sweeter place than Earth as we know it, but Heaven is undoubtedly a physical place. It is just as real as the place where you were born and the place you live today. In fact, Heaven should be capitalized just like Columbus, or Virginia, or France because it is an actual place, more real than any place we have ever been.[3]

The First Christians Believed in Heaven as a Literal Place

The first followers of Jesus believed the Bible taught that Heaven is a genuine, literal, physical place. They always described Heaven in concrete terms as a beautiful, wonderful, joyful, literal, eternal home. Their confidence was obvious. For example, in AD 125, a non-Christian named Aristides wrote to a friend attempting to explain why the new religion called "Christianity" was so successful.

> *If any righteous man among the Christians*
> *passes from this world, they rejoice and offer thanks*
> *to God, and they escort his body with songs and*
> *thanksgiving as if he were setting*
> *from one place to another nearby.*[4]

This belief in Heaven as a literal place continued throughout church history. For example, in the third century a church leader named Cyprian wrote,

> *Who that has been placed in foreign lands*
> *would not hasten to return to his own country? . . .*
> *We regard paradise as our country.*[5]

Throughout the scriptures, Heaven is portrayed as a genuine, actual place. Those who followed the God of the Bible believed in Heaven as real and literal.

Abraham Looked Forward to Living in a Solid City

> *By faith Abraham, when called to go to a place*
> *he would later receive as his inheritance, obeyed*
> *and went, even though he did not know where*
> *he was going. By faith he made his home in the*
> *promised land like a stranger in a foreign coun-*

try; he lived in tents, as did Isaac and Jacob, who
were heirs with him of the same promise. For he
was looking forward to the city with foundations,
whose architect and builder is God.

HEBREWS 11:8–10

Abraham was called by God to leave his homeland and travel to a *place* he had never been (Genesis 12:1). It was a *land* that was promised, but which he did not yet possess. He traveled there by faith and lived there in tents. As he did, he anticipated one day living in another *place,* his heavenly home, a *city* with firm *foundations*, whose architect and builder is God Himself. Abraham viewed Heaven as a literal place, a celestial city. Unlike flimsy, temporary tents, it would have solid, permanent foundations.

The Apostle John Saw Heaven as a Physical Reality

Then I saw a new heaven and a new earth,
for the first heaven and the first earth had passed
away, and there was no longer any sea. I saw the
Holy City, the new Jerusalem, coming down out of
heaven from God, prepared as a bride beautifully
dressed for her husband.

REVELATION 21:1–2

In the book of the Revelation, God gave the apostle John a series of marvelous visions into the future. When John saw into Heaven, he always saw it as a tangible place. In his most extensive vision of Heaven, what John saw was a new Heaven, a new Earth, and a new city—the new Jerusalem. He did not see a *non*-heaven, a *non*-earth, or a *non*-city.

John described Heaven in such detail that what he was seeing had to be more than a ghostly, foggy, ethereal state of being.

John depicted a city with literal walls and tangible gates that were able to be measured (Revelation 21:12–21). It had real streets (21:21). Flowing through the city was a genuine river (22:1–2), bordered with actual trees (22:2). This vision of a literal Heaven was what John was told to write down for us to study, learn, and long for (21:5).

Jesus Promised His Disciples that Heaven Was a Literal Place

> *"Do not let your hearts be troubled. Trust in God; trust also in me. In my Father's house are many rooms; if it were not so, I would have told you. I am going there to prepare a place for you. And if I go and prepare a place for you, I will come back and take you to be with me that you also may be where I am. You know the way to the place where I am going.*
>
> JOHN 14:1–4

Jesus promised His disciples that there would be a literal gathering in an actual place. He deliberately chose clear material terms such as "house," "rooms," and "place." It was a *place* that could be prepared. It was a *place* from which He would go and return. It was a *place* He would take them to so they could be together. It was a *place* to which they had been told the way. Clearly, Jesus wanted His disciples to understand Heaven as being a tangible place.

Jesus Promised the Thief That He Would Join Jesus in Paradise

> *One of the criminals who hung there hurled insults at him: "Aren't you the Christ? Save your-*

> *self and us!" But the other criminal rebuked him.*
> *"Don't you fear God," he said, "since you are*
> *under the same sentence? We are punished justly,*
> *for we are getting what our deeds deserve. But*
> *this man has done nothing wrong." Then he said,*
> *"Jesus, remember me when you come into your*
> *kingdom." Jesus answered him, "I tell you the*
> *truth, today you will be with me in paradise."*
>
> LUKE 23:39–43

As Jesus hung on the cross, the crowd and the soldiers mocked Him. So did one of the criminals being killed alongside Him that day. But the other thief acknowledged God's justice, his own guilt, and Jesus' righteous innocence. Jesus heard the man's statement as a confession of faith and rewarded him with that wonderful promise: "Today you will be with me in paradise."

The word "paradise" describes a beautiful, tangible place. Early Christians understood Paradise as more than mere allegory, but rather as an actual physical place where God lives with His people.

Later, Jesus promised to the overcomers that He would "give the right to eat from the tree of life, which is in the paradise of God" (Revelation 2:7). The tree of life was seen by the apostle John standing by the banks of the river flowing through the city of New Jerusalem (Revelation 22:2). When Jesus told the thief He could join Him in Paradise, He was telling the man about a literal place.

The Resurrection of Jesus Proves That Heaven Is a Physical Reality

The central truth of Christianity is that Jesus rose from the dead with a unique, spiritual body that also had physical dimensions. He was able to be seen, heard, and touched. He ate literal food. More than a ghost, the resurrected Jesus had a visible, tangible, audible, recognizable body. It was a body designed to occupy a literal place, a place not so radically different from Earth as we know it.

Jesus' literal resurrection from the dead not only proved that His death on the cross was sufficient to pay for our sins, but also guaranteed our hope of experiencing eternal life. As the resurrected death destroyer, Jesus is the pioneer, the first one all the way through to the mountain pass. His resurrected body tells us a tremendous amount about the literal nature of Heaven. Although His new, improved body had increased abilities and heightened sensitivities, it was still an actual body. One day all of Jesus' followers will also have similar resurrected bodies. These new, improved bodies are designed for a literal Heaven.

So What?

Heaven is a literal place, so real that everything else we know is mere shadow to its substance. It is a Paradise awaiting those who really want to be there. The rest of this book will describe this glorious place. I pray that as you read of Heaven, it will not only satisfy your curiosity, but feed and fuel your soul to make sure that you will spend eternity there.

NOTES

1.   C. S. Lewis, *The Great Divorce* (New York: Harper Collins, 1946), 21.

2.   Randy C. Alcorn, *Heaven* (Carol Stream, Illinois: Tyndale House Publishers, 2004), xxi.

3.   I agree with Peter Kreeft, "**What Will Heaven Be Like?** Thirty-five frequently asked questions about eternity," Christianity Today (June 6, 2003), http://www.christianitytoday.com/ct/2003/122/51.0.html, that because Heaven is a literal place, it should be capitalized just as we capitalize Boston.

4.   Aristides, *The Apology of Aristides the Philosopher*, 15, http://www.early-christianwritings.com/text/aristides-kay.html.

5.   Cyprian, *On the Mortality*, 26, http://www.newadvent.org/fathers/050707.htm.

"THERE'S NO PLACE LIKE HOME" 2

In 1939 an MGM movie swept American moviegoers away. Shown annually on television during holidays, the movie became a classic institution and a rite of passage for most of us. Interestingly, it is not a bloody war epic, an intrigue-laced detective story, or the tale of a passionate affair. It was the fantastic tale of a girl who ran away—only to find that "there's no place like home."

Kansas farm girl Dorothy Gale felt unnoticed, underappreciated, and lonely. When a nasty neighbor tried to have her little black dog, Toto, put to sleep, young Dorothy scooped Toto into her arms and ran away. A tornado swept up Dorothy, her house, and her dog, depositing them in the magical Land of Oz. She immediately realized that she and Toto weren't in Kansas anymore. Dorothy, in her newly acquired, enchanted, sequined ruby slippers, set out on an adventure down the Yellow Brick Road on a quest to see the only one with the power to help her return home, the wonderful Wizard of Oz.

On her way to the Emerald City, the home of the Wizard, she met a Scarecrow who wanted a brain, a Tin Man who hoped for a heart, and a Cowardly Lion who desperately desired courage. Each hoped to get to the city so the Wizard would help them before the Wicked Witch of the West could catch them.

After an avalanche of adventures, Dorothy discovered that the key to getting home was with her all along. She needed only to close her eyes and tap her heels together three times while thinking, "There's no place like home." When she did, the magic slippers transported her to the place she had so longed to be.

Awakening in her own bed, in her own house, surrounded by the anxious faces of her family and friends, Dorothy made a resolution. She declared, "I will never leave here ever, ever again because. . .there's *no* place like *home.*"

Homesick for Heaven

As they say where I grew up, "Homesick is a bad kind of sick to be." There is no pill you can take to relieve its symptoms. No surgery removes its awful ache. There are temporary distractions, but at best they are still only temporary. The only and ultimate cure for homesickness is going home.

God's children, living life on a groaning planet, live with a gnawing tension and hungry ache for home. There are amazingly good moments in the here and now. Yet, often, life is oddly awkward and uncomfortable. We feel out of step and not quite in sync with "down here." There is holy discontent and persistent inner dissatisfaction. Why? Etched deep into the heart of the Christian is the hunger for Heaven, which is the home we have always longed for.

Heaven is the home you always wanted.

For the Christian, there exists a constant tension between "the here and now" and the "then and there." Even though we have never been there, our spiritual DNA instinctively tells us that our true home is a place we have not yet visited. Our heart is with our treasure, Christ, in heaven (Matthew 6:21; 2 Corinthians 5:8). Heaven is described in the Bible as the home we inwardly desire. To the people of faith described by the author of Hebrews, it was a distant homeland, a country of their own, a better country, a heavenly home.

> *All these people were still living by faith when*
> *they died. They did not receive the things prom-*
> *ised; they only saw them and welcomed them*
> *from a distance. And they admitted that they*
> *were aliens and strangers on earth. People who*
> *say such things show that they are looking for a*
> *country of their own. If they had been thinking*
> *of the country they had left, they would have had*
> *opportunity to return. Instead, they were longing*
> *for a better country—a heavenly one. Therefore*
> *God is not ashamed to be called their God, for he*
> *has prepared a city for them.*
>
> HEBREWS 11:13–16

To the first Christians, the concept of Heaven as the home God's people really desire was so strong that the apostle Peter addressed his first letter "To God's elect, *strangers* in the world. . ." (1 Peter 1:1, emphasis added). In that letter, he encouraged the readers to "live your lives as *strangers* here in reverent fear" (1:17, emphasis added). He used their status as pilgrims on this planet to motivate them to godly living by saying, "Dear friends, I urge you, as *aliens* and *strangers* in the world, to abstain from sinful desires, which war against your soul" (2:11, emphasis added).

"It's Good to Be Home"

Because of the nature of my ministry, I am out of state several times a month, living from a suitcase, speaking at churches or training pastors. I usually fly back into town late at night. Looking out of the window as the plane is drawing down on the airport, there is always a warm sense of the familiar. I can tell I am getting close to where I long to be. Soon Cathy, my wife, is pulling up to the curb and smiling at me as I pile in. After a quick kiss she says, "It's nice to have you home."

Driving down customary streets, time drags until we pull into the driveway. Quickly, I am inside. Rocky, our little dog, dives into me with a flurry of delighted barks. My sons yell out, "Hey Dad, glad you're home," and come by to give me a hug.

Soon, I am lying in my own bed, with my wonderful wife, in my own room, in my own house, with my kids down the hall, on my own street, and all feels well with the world. I give a happy sigh and think, "It's awfully nice to be home."

One day, all of God's children will have that same feeling, multiplied. We will awake and breathe the rich, fresh air of Heaven and sigh, "It is so nice to finally be home."

All the Comforts of Home, Only Better

Think of everything we enjoy about home and realize those elements will be in Heaven, only better, much better. For example, my wife, Cathy, is an outstanding mother. Since our children were born, she has made it a mission that, if nothing else, home was a place of unconditional love and acceptance. The world may give you a rough time, but you can always walk in the door of home and feel received, expected, acknowledged, listened to, and recognized as being valuable.

It will be the same in Heaven, only more so. Rejection, denunciation, and abuse will be unwelcome in Heaven. Genuine affection, fond friendship, and close companionship will reign supreme, and it won't only be in a few rooms with family members. Acceptance and love will be given everywhere you go.

Make Yourself at Home

When you visit good friends, they often encourage you to "make yourself at home." Of course, you never fully do because you are afraid they might never let you come back if you did. But you understand that what they mean is "relax and feel free to be yourself, just as you would at home."

Home is the one place where you can be yourself. You don't have to dress up in uncomfortable clothes and try to impress somebody you really don't know. You can wear a beat-up old sweatshirt if you want (I usually do). You can sing badly in the shower (I am guilty of that one as well). You don't have to comb your hair (I would gladly comb my hair if I had enough to comb).

In Heaven you can kick off your shoes and relax. You can drink right out of the pitcher if you feel like it. You will feel free to be the true you. You will finally be home.

Home-Cooked Meals

We have three teenage sons. One of their favorite things about home is that there is always good food there. Cathy makes the extra effort to bring home their favorite foods and preferred snacks from the grocery store. She is a master at making their best-loved meals and most desired desserts. Yet as good a job as Cathy does with the food in our house, in Heaven we will enjoy even finer food together, as God Himself will be our cook.

> *On this mountain the LORD Almighty will prepare a feast of rich food for all peoples, a banquet of aged wine—the best of meats and the finest of wines.*
>
> ISAIAH 25:6

FFGs

Every few months our family holds an FFG ("Festive Family Gathering"). We come together to celebrate birthdays, graduations, or homecomings from mission trips. My wife and boys are there. Cathy's sister is always there. My sister and her husband never miss. My brother and his wife make it when they can. My parents used to come.

The agenda is simple. We eat and then usually eat a little more. After that we gather in a large room and do a variety of activities. We may sing (usually badly), pray (we are much better at that), and my sister loves to give out goofy "door prizes" (don't even ask). We often give out brutally funny birthday cards. We may look at pictures from someone's mission trip or a video of one of our boy's school events or discuss family business. We always laugh a lot. Our family loves FFGs because they are an excuse to get together and be a family.

Our heavenly home will be filled with FFGs. We will gather with our spiritual brothers and sisters and our heavenly Father, for glorious times of family fun.

Family Feasts

One of the favorite times in our home is family mealtime around the kitchen table. We especially love those rare and wonderful times when Cathy has found steaks on sale at the grocery store and marinated them all day. I grill them outside while she makes salads, vegetables, and all the rest of the fixings. The boys set the table and get the drinks. Someone says grace and we all dig in. Loud laughing punctuates conversations that cover a wide gamut of topics. Everyone is happy because it is good to be home with family.

Don't think this pleasure will be missing in Heaven. Our heavenly home is described as a place of enjoying fantastic feasts together with the ones we love (Matthew 8:11). Jesus promised a rich feast fit for a king for all in Heaven.

> *And I confer on you a kingdom, just as my*
> *Father conferred one on me, so that you may eat*
> *and drink at my table in my kingdom.*
>
> LUKE 22:29–30

Family Is What Makes a House a Home

I grew up in a small yellow house in a small Midwestern town. My folks lived in that same house for over forty years. After I had gone to college and had not been back in months, I will never forget how excited I was to be driving home. When the car turned onto the street and I spotted the tiny yellow house, my heart skipped a beat in anticipation. I was eager to be somewhere familiar. But most of all, I wanted to see the two people that made home "home" for me—Mom and Dad.

Oh, don't get me wrong. Having a room to myself, being done with exams, and having twenty-four-hour access to a refrigerator was deeply appreciated. But that was not what I had missed most. It was Mom and Dad. Yes, eating Mom's home-made apple pie, dining on her special scalloped potatoes, having her do my laundry, and having Dad hand me a twenty-dollar bill was glorious. But I mostly liked being there with them.

A funny thing happened a few months after Dad followed Mom to Heaven. I drove by their old house and, strangely, I felt nothing. What had previously always produced a warm feeling evoked nothing but an eerie void. Their old house was just another house on just another street. Why? My family did not live there anymore. Being together with loved ones is what makes a house a home.

One of the great aspects of our heavenly home is being reunited with loved ones. Yet this reunion will be even better than any family gathering we have ever experienced. Our loved ones will be perfected, and we will be together with them and with the Lord forever.

> *Brothers, we do not want you to be ignorant*
> *about those who fall asleep, or to grieve like the*
> *rest of men, who have no hope. We believe that*
> *Jesus died and rose again and so we believe that*

*God will bring with Jesus those who have fallen
asleep in him. . . . And so we will be with the
Lord forever.*

1 THESSALONIANS 4:13–14, 17

So What?

Maybe you did not have a pleasant home life, or possibly yours was wonderful. Either way, remember that Heaven is the home you always longed for. It will have all the comforts of home and much more. Heaven on its worst day will be better than your home ever was on its best day. Don't get too tied to this Earth, and don't get too frustrated when it fails to meet your expectations. Heaven is the home you have always longed for.

3

PARTYING IN PARADISE

> *If you are not allowed to laugh in Heaven,*
> *I don't want to go there.*
>
> MARTIN LUTHER[1]

Never Underestimate the Power of a Good Party

We all love parties. From little kids getting excited about a birthday party, to teenage boys who finally bathe and use deodorant before going to a party where girls will be attending, to young ladies all atwitter at bridal showers, people love parties. From wedding receptions and anniversaries, to tailgates, getting together with good friends and tasty food is a can't-miss recipe for fun.

Never underestimate the power of a party. My family hosts a weekly Bible study for teens. We have found that we can double our attendance and get unchurched students to come to our house if the kids invite them to a "party." We have found if we have a theme ("Squirt Gun Wars," "I Hate Winter," "Halloween Bonfire," and "Fifties Night" are always hits), grill some hot dogs, and play a few corny games, we'll have a crowd. They will have a blast and will listen intently to a few of their friends share their story of how they came to a personal relationship with Jesus. We have had as many as eighty-nine kids show up and as many as a dozen make salvation decisions for Christ—all because we had a party.

"No, I Don't Want to Go to Heaven. Heaven Is Boring, and I Love to Party."

Several years ago I was talking with a young man. In the course of our conversation, I asked him if he would like to know how to go to Heaven. "No!" he said, shaking his head. "I don't want to go to Heaven. Heaven is so boring and I just love to party."

Some of the saddest misconceptions the devil has spread about God and Heaven are that "God hates fun" and "Heaven is boring." Nothing could be further from the truth! God is the absolutely, positively most exciting Being in the universe. Where God is, parties break out. If you *like* parties, you will *love* Heaven.

Heaven is the home of the best parties ever.

God Loves a Good Party

In the Bible, God went out of His way to tell His people that He wanted them to have parties on Earth. These parties certainly weren't drunken, but they were fun gatherings with great amounts of good food, good friends, and good times. For example, in the seemingly unlikely, widely viewed as "dull as dust" book of Deuteronomy, God commands His people to have an annual national celebration.

> *Be sure to set aside a tenth of all that your fields produce each year. Eat the tithe of your grain, new wine and oil, and the firstborn of your herds and flocks in the presence of the LORD your God at the place he will choose as a dwelling for his Name, so that you may learn to revere the LORD your God always. But if that place is too distant and you have been blessed by the LORD your God and cannot carry your tithe (because the place where the LORD will choose to put his*

Name is so far away), then exchange your tithe
for silver, and take the silver with you and go to
the place the LORD your God will choose. Use the
silver to buy whatever you like: cattle, sheep, wine
or other fermented drink, or anything you wish.
Then you and your household shall eat there in
the presence of the LORD your God and rejoice.

DEUTERONOMY 14:22–26

The first time I read that passage I thought, "This is the very best tithing text I have ever heard! Why didn't anyone tell me this was in the Bible?"

Note carefully what it is saying. The Jewish law stated that every year all Jewish families were to gather up one-tenth of their crops from that year and bring them to Jerusalem. What were they to do with all of that? Were they to feed the poor, clothe the naked, or possibly add a family life center onto the temple? No, they were to use it to have a humongous party!

This was to be an amazing celebration. Everyone would be there. Farmers, merchants, family leaders, large families, soldiers, priests, grandmas, and little kids, widows, orphans, lame people, the blind—everyone was welcome. No one was excluded. There would be plenty of food, singing, and lots of fun. And it would all be done to honor God.

The Lord was honored by their party! Our God is a God who loves celebration. He is a God whose very presence breathes joy into living. God loves a good party.

God loves parties so much that He commanded His children to take time off work and to faithfully enjoy parties together. He even ordained that the entire Jewish religious calendar be based on national parties or "feasts." If God prescribed parties such as the following for inclusion in the Jewish calendar, don't you think He'll have them in Heaven?

1. The Feast of Dedication was held in the winter month of Chisleu (John 10:22).

2. The Feast of Jubilee was proclaimed by trumpets every fiftieth year (Leviticus 25:8–12).

3. The Feast of the New Moon was to be observed the first day of every month with trumpets (Numbers 10:10) and entertainment (1 Samuel 20:5, 18).

4. The Feast of Pentecost (also called the Feast of Harvest or the Feast of Weeks) was to be kept fifty days after the barley harvest with great rejoicing (Leviticus 23:15–16; Deuteronomy 16:9–12).

5. The Feast of Purim or Lots was commemorated on the fourteenth and fifteenth days of the twelfth month with feasting, gladness, and the sharing of gifts (Esther 9:17–22).

6. Feast of the Sabbatical Year was to be celebrated every seventh year (Leviticus 25:2–7; Exodus 23:11).

7. The Feast of Tabernacles was a joyous, weeklong annual feast of singing and camping out (Exodus 23:16–17; Leviticus 23:34–41; Deuteronomy 16:13–15).

8. The Feast of the Passover (or Feast of Unleavened Bread) was also an annual week-long feast (Exodus 12:6–18; Leviticus 23:5–6).

9. The Feast of Trumpets was held the first day of the seventh month (Leviticus 23:24–25; Numbers 29:1–6).

10. The Anniversary Feasts (Exodus 23:14–16) were to be times of gratitude, joy, gladness, and entertainment (Psalm 122:4; 42:4; 1 Samuel 1:4–9).

Jesus Loves a Good Party

Q: Where did Jesus do His first miracle?
A: At a wedding party (John 2:1–10)

Q: Where was Jesus anointed for His burial?
A: At a dinner party (Luke 7:36–50)

Q: Where did Jesus eat His last meal with His disciples?
A: At a supper party (Matthew 26:17–30)

Q: What did Jesus say happens in the presence of God when a sinner repents?
A: The Father throws a party (Luke 15:5–7, 9–10, 22–24).

> *"When he finds [his lost sheep], he joyfully puts it on his shoulders and goes home. Then he calls his friends and neighbors together and says, 'Rejoice with me; I have found my lost sheep.' I tell you that in the same way there will be more rejoicing in heaven over one sinner who repents than over ninety-nine righteous persons who do not need to repent."*
>
> LUKE 15:5–7

"When she finds [her lost coin], she calls her friends and neighbors together and says, 'Rejoice with me; I have found my lost coin.' In the same way, I tell you, there is rejoicing in the presence of the angels of God over one sinner who repents."

LUKE 15:9–10

"'Quick! Bring the best robe and put it on him. Put a ring on his finger and sandals on his feet. Bring the fattened calf and kill it. Let's have a feast and celebrate. For this son of mine was dead and is alive again; he was lost and is found.' So they began to celebrate. Meanwhile, the older son was in the field. When he came near the house, he heard music and dancing."

LUKE 15:22–25

I absolutely love this. When I lead people to Jesus, I tell them that they cannot possibly fathom the profound, life-changing importance of the commitment they made. "It is so significant," I say, "that this very moment the Father, the Son, and the Holy Spirit, the angels, and a whole bunch of people like your godly great grandma are 'high-fiving,' dancing, and laughing. They are having a party in your honor, in the honor of one day having you join them in Heaven, and in the honor of Jesus Christ, who died to make it possible!"

In our church, we celebrate baptism once a month. Those who have trusted Christ as Savior the previous month have their testimonies read out loud before they are baptized. When they come up out of the water, everyone in the audience breaks into clapping and cheering. It's a mini-party.

Q: Why did the Pharisees get so upset with Jesus?
A: He was too interested in parties (Luke 7:34).

> *"The Son of Man came eating and drinking,*
> *and you say, 'Here is a glutton and a drunkard, a*
> *friend of tax collectors and "sinners."*

Luke 7:34

Pharisees were the "no-fun" bunch in Jesus' day. They consistently valued man-made rules over eternal relationships. They loved their policies more than people. Jesus gave them fits. He refused to make religion a dull, dry, rigid, sober, stupefying act. He was obviously a very holy person who connected with people and knew how to have fun with them. He frequented the parties of "sinners," prostitutes, and tax collectors in order to bring light into their darkness.

Q: To what did Jesus compare the kingdom of Heaven?
A: A big-time banquet (Luke 14:15–24)

Jesus was the master storyteller. He told simple stories with profound meaning. In one He compares Heaven with a great banquet.

> *When one of those at the table with him heard*
> *this, he said to Jesus, "Blessed is the man who will*
> *eat at the feast in the kingdom of God."*
> *Jesus replied: "A certain man was preparing*
> *a great banquet and invited many guests. At the*
> *time of the banquet he sent his servant to tell those*
> *who had been invited, 'Come, for everything is*

now ready.'

"But they all alike began to make excuses. The first said, 'I have just bought a field, and I must go and see it. Please excuse me.'

"Another said, 'I have just bought five yoke of oxen, and I'm on my way to try them out. Please excuse me.'

"Still another said, 'I just got married, so I can't come.'

"The servant came back and reported this to his master. Then the owner of the house became angry and ordered his servant, 'Go out quickly into the streets and alleys of the town and bring in the poor, the crippled, the blind and the lame.'"

"'Sir,' the servant said, 'what you ordered has been done, but there is still room.'

"Then the master told his servant, 'Go out to the roads and country lanes and make them come in, so that my house will be full. I tell you, not one of those men who were invited will get a taste of my banquet.'"

LUKE 14:15–24

Jesus told this tale to teach us about God's huge heart of love for hurting, helpless people and something of His nature as the heavenly host with the most. In this story, Jesus teaches five truths about Heaven.

1. Heaven will host a feast of fulfillment and happiness: *Blessed is the man who will eat at the feast in the kingdom of God* (Luke 14:15).

2. Heaven is being prepared as a great banquet: *A certain man was preparing a great banquet* (Luke 14:16).

3. Heaven is a celebration where misplaced priorities may prohibit entrance: *But they all alike began to make excuses. The first said, "I have just bought a field, and I must go and see it. Please excuse me." Another said, "I have just bought five yoke of oxen, and I'm on my way to try them out. Please excuse me." Still another said, "I just got married, so I can't come."* . . .*Then the master told his servant, "I tell you, not one of those men who were invited will get a taste of my banquet"* (Luke 14:18–20, 23–24).

4. Heaven is a blessed bash where supposed liabilities are overlooked: *Go out quickly into the streets and alleys of the town and bring in the poor, the crippled, the blind and the lame* (Luke 14:21).

5. Heaven is large enough to accommodate all who really want to be there: *Go out to the roads and country lanes and make them come in, so that my house will be full* (Luke 14:23).

So What?

This very moment God is preparing a party in Heaven. An invitation has been sent to you. I hope you will accept. We could have a great time together in Heaven.

NOTES

1. Martin Luther Quotes, Brainy Quotes, http://www.brainyquote.com/quotes/authors/m/martin_luther.html.

4

NOT EVEN CLOSE TO BORING

I was an active little boy who was easily bored. During my days in elementary school, I spent many hours standing in the corner or visiting with our principal, Mr. Crabtree, not because I was "bad" as much as because I was too "busy" and easily bored.

I remember leaving Sunday school one morning in a real dilemma. I knew I should want to go to Heaven, but it sounded so b–o–r–i–n–g. The thought of playing harps and singing hymns all day, every day, forever did nothing to capture my attention. It sounded like choir practice, which was fine once a week, but having it all the time, every week, year after year, century after century—boring!

No Yawns Allowed

Q: What happens in hell?
A: Nothing
Q: What happens in Heaven?
A: Everything[1]

Studying what the Bible says about Heaven has produced the definite resolution of my dilemma regarding the supposedly dull nature of Heaven. I no longer wonder about being restless in Heaven, because Heaven is the most exciting place in the universe. Being in Heaven is called eternal *life*, not endless boredom. Heaven will pulsate with life and vibrancy. It is an active, fun, peaceful, positive, adventurous place.

Heaven is the most exciting place in the universe.

God Is the Most Exhilarating Person in the Universe

God has many characteristics, but none of them are boring. God is unparalleled regarding creativity, unrivaled regarding riches, and untouched in terms of power. He is the inventor of miracles and the fulfiller of dreams. He is the Author of *life,* for crying out loud!

No accurate description of God can contain any words like *dead, dry, dull, dreary, lackluster, lethargic,* or *lifeless. Electrifying, exciting, exhilarating, stirring, thrilling, dynamic, lively, active, vigorous,* and *vibrant* are just a few adjectives that anyone who truly knows God would use to describe Him. The people who have lived the most adventuresome and adrenaline-laced lives are the ones who have lived closest to Him.

Remember David, the shepherd boy? By being associated with God, he got to bring down a real giant, chase Philistines, avoid an entire army, rule a kingdom, and dance before the Lord in unbridled, uninhibited joy. His closest companions were fearless warriors called "Mighty Men," not "Boring Boys." Nobody could call them, or their life experiences, dull.

What about Daniel? He served on the cabinet of several world rulers, was miraculously delivered from death by lions, and was privileged to see a vision of the future equaled only by one other man, John the apostle.

How about Elijah? He and God single-handedly caused a three-year drought, miraculously fed a widow and her son, and defeated 850 false prophets. He called down real fire from

Heaven and took a ride to Heaven in a flaming chariot chauffeured by angels. Boring? You have to be kidding.

Ponder the exciting perils of Paul. His introduction to Jesus began when he was knocked off his horse by a blinding light. Knowing Jesus forced him to flee for his life over a wall in a basket. Being close to God led Paul in and out of jail, before adoring and lethally angry crowds, into the presence of kings, through earthquakes and shipwrecks, and to travel around the known world. Because of God, Paul healed the sick and raised the dead. There was nothing routine and monotonous about his life.

Talk to the original disciples. They will tell you that by hanging around with Jesus they saw the lame walk, the blind see, the dead live, storms stop, and thousands of hungry people fed with a handful of food, twice.

Any view of God that contains the notion of boredom is an absolute lie. Such lies are exploded the moment people experience the thrilling nature of His home, Heaven.

God Created Us to Live Anything but Boring Lives

I often tell audiences, "If you are living a boring Christian life, don't blame God!" I have found that truly following Jesus is anything but dull. It is definitely not easy, but it is also never boring. Following Jesus will force us out of our comfort zone.

Convenience and complacency flee in the face of the courage and creativity required to pursue and obey Christ. Following Jesus will push us out of the security of the boat to walk on water and out onto the battlefield to face giants. People who think Christianity is boring ought to try it the way it was meant to be lived. And people who think that Heaven is dull ought to read the Bible.

Daily Life in Heaven

Daily life in Heaven will be similar to daily life on Earth, only much more fun and fulfilling. God created humans with an immense capacity to experience pleasure, adventure, fun, and joy. In Heaven this capacity will not only be greatly expanded, it will also be powerfully purified and gloriously satisfied.

Remember, the curse will be lifted (Revelation 22:3). Therefore, everything good, pleasant, and truly fun about Heaven will be better than it ever could be here on Earth.

Dining Will Be Delightful

We will eat better-tasting, more exotic, much healthier, and more delicious foods than are available on Earth now under the curse (Isaiah 25:6). I see creative chefs, remarkable recipes, and awe-inspiring menus. We will be able to dine with good people who love us, as well as with fascinating people we have always wanted to meet.

Travel Will Be Tremendous

Travel will be incredible in Heaven. Ultimately, the new Earth will be every bit as beautiful as Earth is now, and even better. We will have all of eternity to explore mountains, nations, islands, and other places we have never had the time or money to see. We can discover marvelous museums, glorious art galleries, and look at extraordinary architecture. Beyond that, why won't we be able to visit the sights on other planets, stars, galaxies, and solar systems? There will be practically no end to where we can go and what we can see.

Work Will Be Wonderful

Although it is not necessarily the case on Earth now under the curse, work will be a great joy in Heaven. Everyone in Heaven will serve in positions they thoroughly enjoy, doing work that is meaningful and deeply fulfilling. It will stretch us and we will love it. We will work alongside great companions and serve a wonderful Boss (Revelation 22:3).

Worship Won't Put You to Sleep

One of the great misconceptions about Heaven is that it will be one infinitely long, dreadfully brain-numbing, boring church service. According to the Bible, there will be a lot of worship in Heaven, but don't worry. It will be better than anything you have ever been a part of. I can guarantee you, it will be vastly superior to the shot made at the buzzer of the championship game, bigger than the best concert, and a cut above the most peaceful sunset.

Unlike too much of what some call worship on Earth, in Heaven there will be absolutely no lifeless singing, no dry prayers, no passionless preaching, and no looking at the clock and wondering what is for lunch. Worship in Heaven will be so thoroughly captivating it will be unlike any worship you have ever experienced down here under the curse.

Heavenly worship will elevate you out of yourself and shake you down to your core. It will drain you and flood you, lift you up, and drop you to your knees. It will strike every emotional chord you have ever felt and many you did not even know you had. You will cry, laugh, cheer, and shudder. Every negative emotion inside you will be swept aside in tidal waves of raw joy, holy happiness, deep awe, extreme peace, and outrageous love. It will fully engage all five senses and possibly enliven new senses that did not exist previously. Boring? No way!

For example, the book of Revelation is more than an amazing book of prophecy telling us of coming events. It is also a glorious glimpse into a few of the wonderful worship events in Heaven. The word "throne" appears over forty times in Revelation, often in the context of the staggering events God's people will experience worshiping around His throne. From looking at just a few of them, I can tell you that when you worship in Heaven it will be anything but boring.

Imagine every color in the rainbow ignited and exploding

before your eyes (Revelation 4:2–3). Feel rocked to your core by the thunder, lightning, and sea of voices roaring in perfect syncopation and symphony around the throne (4:5). Drink in stunning splendor and spectacular beauty (4:6), and witness astounding angelic creatures (4:7–9). By worshiping directly at the throne of the Author of life, you become more alive than you ever imagined possible (4:9–11).

As you worship in Heaven, you will cry like a baby (5:4) and be comforted by astounding truth (5:5). Your breath will be swept away as you see Jesus as He has never been seen before (5:6–7) and find within your heart a river of gratitude beyond what you conceived possible. Such experiences will pull the very best out of your entire life and present it to Him (5:8).

At the throne, you will sing in tune and perfect pitch in a choir of millions of voices, including people from every epoch in history, every nation on earth, and every station of life, each tuned perfectly to one another and to the Lord (5:9–10). Billions of angels will join you at the throne in celestial crescendos that defy description (5:11–12). Ultimately, every animal, every fish, and every bird will join you in jubilant praise and worship of their creator King (5:13–14). Think about it: You may be standing behind a regal Ethiopian warrior and in front of a Polish grandma, together proclaiming God's worth, with an enormous glowing angel on one side and a happy polar bear on the other.

But if all of that is not enough, imagine the righteous pride exploding in your chest for Jesus as every evil, dirty, slithering demon and the dark prince himself, Satan, bow down before Jesus. Hear them sheepishly acknowledge the truth they have lived to deny, as they finally proclaim, "Jesus is Lord!" (Revelation 5:13–14; Philippians 2:9–11)

Friend, if that does not send shivers down your spine and cause goose bumps to spread down your arms, call 911. For all practical purposes, you are dead.

So What?

After studying the enthralling adventure of Heaven, I no longer fear that anyone will be bored. Actually, my greatest concern is that many Christians I know who are in the habit of going through the motions will be so energized, keyed up, and enthused by the thrilling atmosphere of Heaven that they will not survive, unless God performs a major miracle.

My goal is to live the adventure now. I want to have my heart, mind, and soul stretched so far by loving God and serving Him that Heaven won't be such a big shock to my system. I want to be well prepared to completely comprehend it and entirely enjoy it all when I get there.

NOTES

1.   Peter Kreeft, **"What Will Heaven Be Like?** *Thirty-five frequently asked questions about eternity,"* Christianity Today (06/06/2003), http://www.christianitytoday.com/ct/2003/122/51.0.html.

A MUCH BETTER PLACE

5

When I was a very young boy, my grandfather passed away. He had a habit of telling the same jokes over and over again, so we called him "Granddaddy Joke." My brother and I considered Granddaddy Joke our favorite grandfather, because he gave us big bowls of pink peppermint ice cream when we visited him and tickled us with his stubbly face. (Our other grandfather always put us to work when we visited him.)

As we were riding in the hearse from the funeral service to the cemetery, everyone in my family was silent except for sniffles and sobs. Finally, I could not take it anymore.

"Why are we all crying?" I asked, as my childish mind grappled with the weighty issue of mortality and the puzzling nature of grief.

"We should be happy. Granddaddy Joke's in Heaven, and Heaven is a much better place, right?"

My appreciation for the pain of grief was obviously underdeveloped, but my theology was quite good. Heaven is a much better place than Earth as we now know it.

**Heaven on its worst day is better
than Earth on its best day.**

*Then I saw a new heaven and a new
earth. . . . And I heard a loud voice from the throne
saying, "Now the dwelling of God is with men, and*

> *he will live with them. They will be his people,*
> *and God himself will be with them and be their*
> *God. He will wipe every tear from their eyes.*
> *There will be no more death or mourning or cry-*
> *ing or pain, for the old order of things has passed*
> *away." He who was seated on the throne said, "I*
> *am making everything new!"*
>
> REVELATION 21:1, 3–5

Heaven will be a much better place than Earth for many reasons. It will ultimately be a new and vastly improved version (Revelation 21:1). God will ultimately wipe away every tear (21:4). Death will be eradicated (21:4). Heaven is vastly superior to the Earth we now inhabit. In Heaven everything good about Earth will be refreshed, expanded, and enhanced (21:5). Everything bad about it will be absent.

There Is No Sin in Heaven

One major element that will make Heaven "heavenly" is that the curse of sin will be left far behind (Revelation 22:3). The transformational power of Jesus' death, burial, and resurrection for our sin will be experienced on a much greater level than we can now comprehend. Sin's penalty will be paid, its power broken, and its presence completely removed. There is no sin in Heaven.

Sin is breaking God's law. In Heaven there is no sin (Romans 6:14). Therefore, no one will break the law. In other words, there will be no bad people in Heaven (Revelation 21:8; 22:15). No one will steal, rob, rape, or murder. You will not need to fear being abused, molested, assaulted, mugged, or kidnapped. You won't have to lock the doors when you leave. Security systems and fences will be unnecessary. No one will need to carry a gun. Mace and pepper spray will be missing.

In Heaven there will be no need for courtrooms, jails, dungeons, or prisons, because there will be no criminals. The role of judges, lawyers, and police officers will be unnecessary or will radically change.

I am not sure about the role, if any, for policemen in Heaven. During the Welsh Revival of 1904, God's presence was incredibly thick in Wales for a period of months. In twelve months on that tiny land, one hundred thousand people were saved and many others' spirits were revived. As a result, crime all but ceased. The courts and jails were deserted, and the police found themselves without any work to do. The story is told of policemen who closed their station and formed a choir to sing at the revival meetings.

Sin is moral crookedness. There will be no perversion, moral filth, or corruption in Heaven. Pornography, prostitution, drug dealing, and sexual abuse will have no role in Heaven. The media, if there is need for one, will be pure, positive, and powerfully encouraging. There will be no bad news to report. Nothing will fly out over the airwaves or appear on a printed page that would dishonor God or offend His people.

Sin is rebellion. In the new Heaven, there will be no need of a military presence to put down uprisings. Soldiers will have no one to fight. Peace will rule.

Sin is straying off God's course and following the wrong path. Satan worshipers, false teachers, fortune tellers, witches, and psychics will have no home in Heaven (Revelation 22:15).

Sin is missing God's mark. In Heaven moral, spiritual, mental, emotional, and physical potential will be realized. Instead of focusing on illness and disease, heath care persons can help us maximize health and nutrition. There will be no disease. There are no negatives in Heaven.

There Will Be No Untransformed "Sinners" in Heaven

I am quite certain that there will be "sinners" in Heaven—after all, I plan on being there. In fact, Heaven will be full of "sinners," or, more accurately, "*ex*-sinners." Former thieves, liars, murderers, and adulterers will abound. Didn't Jesus tell the thief on the cross he would join Jesus in Paradise (Luke 23:43)? Didn't Paul describe himself as the worst of sinners (1 Timothy 1:15)?

The human luminaries in Heaven will be a "who's who" of people with a past. Moses *was* a murderer. So *was* David. Joshua *had been* cowardly and initially lacked faith. So *did* Gideon, Moses, and Thomas. Rahab *was* a harlot. Bathsheba *was* an adulteress. Judah and David *were* adulterers. Mary Magdalene *had been* a very "loose woman." Solomon *had* three hundred concubines. He also *had* married hundreds of pagan women who turned his heart from the Lord.

Abraham and Jacob *had* terrible troubles with lying. Noah *had* a drinking problem. Miriam *was* a gossip. Jonah *ran* from God. Martha *was* a work-addicted worrier. Mary *might have been* a bit lazy. James and John *wrestled* with selfish ambition. Peter *denied* Jesus. The disciples *hid*. Mark *was* a quitter.

Every human in Heaven will have a past as a "sinner." All will be an ex-something (replace *something* with words like "liar," "drunk," "thief," "cheat," "gossip," "doubter," "glutton"). But, unlike people now on Earth, that sinful part of our personality will be gone, washed away forever by the power of the crucified blood of the Lord Jesus Christ. Our personalities will be transformed into what they were originally intended to be before the world, the flesh, and the devil twisted them into something hideous and grotesquely evil. They will be a glorious reflection of the character of the Lord Jesus. So, even though there will be "sinners" in Heaven, we will become gloriously transformed saints.

Heaven will be a much better place. You will like yourself and others much better because all our sinful tendencies will be gone.

You Will Like Yourself Much Better in Heaven

One of the big reasons I committed my life completely to following Jesus Christ is because a long time ago I realized that I could never escape "me." I have to be with "me" 24/7. There is no place I can go on this planet to flee from myself. Therefore, I had better enjoy the person I am becoming. Other people will not always like me, but I had better be able to appreciate and respect the person I am.

One of the aspects of Heaven I am most thrilled about is I'll be the very best "me" I can be. Self-centeredness, selfish ambition, and selfishness will no longer be enemies I must constantly fight. Fear, doubt, dread, worry, and anxiety will not limit me. Bitterness, resentment, and anger will not have to be continually rooted out of my heart. Greed, lust, jealousy, and envy won't try to capture my heart.

You Will Enjoy People Much More in Heaven

I have to confess, I have a hard time loving, or even liking, some Christian people. Some are hard to like because they have chosen to become so incredibly dull or dreary. There are those who are far too narrow-minded and others who are too open-minded. Some I struggle to love because they rub me the wrong way, their battles with sin correspond too closely with my own. Others have hurts, hang-ups, or habits that have so tainted their lives they are very hard to love.

However, I am sure I won't have any trouble enjoying the company of every single person in Heaven. Pride, arrogance, pettiness, jealousy, and self-righteousness will be gloriously absent from their personalities. . .and mine. The deep wounds that turned them into hurtful people will be gloriously healed in Heaven.

There Is No Curse in Heaven

Just as sin will be removed, its consequences will be eradicated from Heaven (Revelation 22:3). Prior to sin staining Earth, it was a paradise of perfect peace, ideal innocence, and complete community. Since sin entered the world, our universe has lived under the curse of the consequences of sin. Everything has been tainted, stained, twisted, and cheapened.

Prior to sin, in the Garden of Eden the perfect atmosphere produced wonderful weather. There were no natural disasters. Floods, storms, gales, tempests, tornadoes, cyclones, typhoons, whirlwinds, twisters, squalls, hurricanes, blizzards, whiteouts, blackouts, and monsoons did not exist. Heaven will be like that, but even better. The land, air, and water will be perfectly pure. There will be absolutely no trace of pollution, smog, contamination, toxic waste, or trash.

In Heaven the human, plant, and animal kingdoms will live together in absolute harmony. Snakes will not be poisonous. (They also won't tempt us to sin.) If there are any mosquitoes, they will not bite humans. Raccoons won't tip over garbage cans. Termites won't eat the porch. Bees won't sting. Dogs won't bite. I am guessing that even cats will be nice, that is if cats make it to Heaven (just kidding!).

The environment will be pleasantly perfect in Heaven. There will be no frostbite. My balding head won't get sunburned. The disturbing nightmares that often come on full-moon nights won't happen in Heaven.

No germs or viruses will exist in Heaven. *Disease, illness, sickness, infirmity*, and *infection* will drop out of our dictionaries. So will terms such as *ailment, disorder, malady*, and *affliction*.

What will scientists, doctors, dentists, pharmacists, opticians, nurses, and surgeons do in Heaven? My guess is that they will focus on studying health and helping us maximize the potential of our new bodies. What about psychologists, psychiatrists, and counselors? If those jobs exist in any form, I assume that they will help us maximize our mental and emotional potential.

Don't plan on seeing hospitals, sanatoriums, nursing homes, rehab centers, or clinics in Heaven. There definitely will be no morgues, funeral homes, or cemeteries. Heaven is all about life, and death will not exist (Revelation 21:4).

So What?

Knowing that Heaven is a much better place than Earth makes me long for Heaven. It also gives me patience with the imperfections of Earth, knowing that they will largely be forgotten in the superior perfections of Heaven.

THE WORLD'S GREATEST
FAMILY REUNION

*None of those earthly family reunions, however,
prepared me for the sublime gathering of saints I
experienced at the gates of heaven.*

DON PIPER[1]

"I Will See Them on the Other Side"

In January 2006 the tiny town of Tallmansville, West Virginia, was rocked when an explosion in the Sago Mine left twelve miners trapped underground to die of toxic gases. Some of the twelve scrawled farewell notes to their loved ones. One, Martin Toler, Jr., known as "JR," wrote these words, "Tell them all I will see them on the other side. . .I love you."[2]

"I will see them on the other side." One of the most anticipated aspects of Heaven is the assurance of being reunited with friends and family who have gone on before us. Heaven hosts a happy and continual series of fantastic family reunions.

**Heaven is the home of the most, the biggest,
and the best reunions imaginable.**

"The World's Largest Family Reunion"

One of the most notorious family feuds in history was finally put to rest in the summer of 2000. The rivalries between the Hatfields and the McCoys began boiling in 1863 and continued off and on for nearly thirty years. The true origin of the feud between these two families is lost in the mists of history, but legend has it that bitter feelings became violent in 1878 when Randolph McCoy accused Floyd Hatfield of stealing one of his hogs. In total, the feud claimed the lives of twelve men.

Descendants of these famous families saw lingering effects disappear at the first ever Hatfield and McCoy national reunion held in June 2000 in Pikeville, Kentucky, and Matewan, West Virginia. The "truce signing" ceremony was aired on national television.

Today, the reunion claims to be "The World's Largest Family Reunion." It has grown into a full-blown festival spread across three counties and into two states (Kentucky and West Virginia) complete with corporate sponsors and news media in attendance. It features heated "rematches" between the Hatfields and the McCoys in a "friendly" game of softball and a tug-of-war across the appropriately named Tug River. The festival covers several busy days and includes free concerts, a live dramatic reenactment of the feud, a golf tournament, a street fair, a carnival, an ATV ride, and a marathon.

The Hatfield and McCoy reunion has become quite elaborate, very large, and a great deal of fun—but it is nothing compared to the family reunions to be staged in Heaven. It's estimated that twenty million family members gather at some four hundred thousand reunion events each year. But they will not compare with the intensity and joy of the family reunions in Heaven. In Heaven the food will be better, the fun purer, the joy deeper, and the good times endless.

Heaven, God's Forever Family Reunion

God's family reunion is open to all who have been born again by faith in Jesus Christ. God loves us and deeply desires to have us in His family. He loves us so much that He gave His Son to die on the cross to pay for our sins. His death provides us with the gift of eternal life. When we place faith in Jesus Christ, we are born again into God's forever family.

Yet to all who received him, to those who
believed in his name, he gave the right to become
children of God—children born not of natural
descent, nor of human decision or a husband's will,
but born of God.

JOHN 1:12–13

As God's children, we relate to Him as our Father (Matthew 6:9; Romans 8:15; Galatians 4:6), to Jesus as our brother (Romans 8:17; Hebrews 2:11), and to one another as siblings (Galatians 6:10). In one sense, we will relate to everyone in Heaven as family.

Ninety Minutes in Heaven

Don Piper's car was crushed by a semi truck that crossed into his lane. Medical personnel said he died instantly. While his body lay lifeless inside the ruins of his car, Piper experienced the glories of Heaven, awed by its beauty and music. Ninety minutes after the wreck, while a minister prayed for him, Piper miraculously returned to life on earth with only the memory of inexpressible heavenly bliss.[3]

Piper's memory of his ninety minutes in Heaven was of intense joy created by indescribably beautiful music, warm wonderful light, an immense shimmering gate, and a welcoming committee. The heavenly welcome wagon was made up of all the people who had played a role in Piper's spiritual journey. They displayed extreme delight that he was joining them. One by one they hugged him and touched him with the profoundest level of pure affection and love Don had ever experienced. He never felt more welcome and at home.

There are many tales of near-death experiences that I do not accept as true because they don't correspond with what the Bible says about death and Heaven—but not so Piper's. His story of ninety minutes in Heaven rings true when compared to the Bible.

I am not sure everyone will have exactly the same experience as his, but I do believe we will be graciously greeted by our spiritual brothers and sisters who have gone on before us.

United with the Father

In one sense, just arriving in Heaven will create a festive family union. We will be united with our Heavenly family as the prodigal son was with his family (Luke 15:11–24). I think that every time one of us arrives in heaven, the Father, seeing us coming from a long way off, will run to us, hug our necks, and kiss us (Luke 15:20). We will be delighted not to see His face *again,* but to see it for the very first time. While we are broken by His uninhibited expression of unconditional love to undeserving sinners, He will brush our apologies aside and call for a celebration.

Joy will burst out like the sun. First, He will tell the angels (possibly our guardian angels) to bring the best robe and put it on our shoulders, place the family ring on our finger, and put sandals on our feet (Luke 15:22). Then Father will have the fatted calf slaughtered and call our brothers and sisters to eat with us, be merry, and celebrate our arrival (Luke 15:23). Being a very wealthy Father, our arrival party could last days, or even weeks. Yet not one will want to leave because of the joy of having us there finally at home.

The celebration in Heaven will not be because we have *returned* home, but because we have finally *arrived* home. We will share the family name, likeness, and history with everyone in Heaven. If not a family *re*-union, it will be a family union. It will surpass any earthly family reunion ever held, in terms of ebullient joy, extreme love, and expressive celebration.

Spiritual Family Reunions

Paul told the believers in Thessalonica and Philippi he was eager to join together with them before Jesus in Heaven.

> *For what is our hope, our joy, or the crown in*
> *which we will glory in the presence of our Lord Jesus*
> *when he comes? Is it not you?*
>
> 1 THESSALONIANS 2:19

> *Therefore, my brothers, you whom I love and*
> *long for, my joy and crown, that is how you should*
> *stand firm in the Lord, dear friends!*
>
> PHILIPPIANS 4:1

In Heaven we will be reunited with *spiritual* family members. As an adult, I would love to be able to sufficiently thank the three men who pastored my church when I was growing up. Only now am I able to truly appreciate their sacrifices and hard work.

I have had the privilege of leading people to Christ in distant states and other countries, whom I have never seen again. In Heaven we will have time and opportunity for them to tell me of their spiritual journeys. As a pastor, many of my sheep moved on to other states, and I have not seen them since. It will be a treat to catch up with them in Heaven. I will have great joy as I hear how my children walked in truth (3 John 4).

Heavenly Family Reunions

Last year our family went on a cruise. We were surprised by the number of families celebrating reunions on the cruise. They wore brightly colored T-shirts emblazoned with messages such as "Smith Family Reunion 2005."

While earthly family reunions can be big and fun, heavenly ones will be even bigger and better. In Heaven we will be reunited with biological family members who have gone on before us. As I have mentioned previously, I deeply long to see my mom and dad again. Cathy and I look forward to seeing her father again. My grandparents and most of my aunts and uncles are already there;

it will be interesting to see them again. It will also be fascinating to meet family members who knew the Lord and went to Heaven hundreds and even thousands of years ago.

Maybe the thought of a family reunion gives you the creeps. Maybe you have some odd, ornery, or annoying family members whom you would rather not spend eternity with. Let me remind you, our sin natures stay behind when we go to Heaven. All of us will be our very best selves. We will be more patient and loving, and our family members will be more like Christ as well. Family reunions in Heaven will be heavenly.

Maybe your family has been fractured by divorce, division, or distance. Those who are Christians will lay aside every difference and be reunited in Heaven to sign a permanent truce. They may enjoy a "friendly game of softball" or a low-key tug-of-war.

Possibly you are the only Christian in your family. May the notion of heavenly family reunions motivate you to continue to pray for and witness to your loved ones. You have nothing to lose and everything to gain. Cathy and I have worked hard to make sure our children have a growing, personal relationship with Jesus. We want to be sure we can share Heaven together as a family.

The 65th Troop Carrier

One of the highlights of my parents' later years was the semiannual reunion of the 65th Troop Carrier Squadron of the U.S. Army Air Force. Dad and his cronies who served together in the Philippines in World War II, along with their wives, loved to gather in various parts of the country for a weekend of food, fun, and the retelling of old stories. Every six months a different veteran hosted the group in his hometown. Group size ranged from twenty to nearly a hundred.

They shared a special bond, having endured the Great Depression as a generation and, especially, because they had endured the hardships of war as a unit. The more they met together, the deeper their love for each other grew.

In Heaven there will be reunions of spiritual soldiers. I can picture David's Mighty Men manhandling a massive meal and reliving their exciting exploits (2 Samuel 23:8–39). Shadrach, Meshach, and Abednego could get together to celebrate the annual anniversary of the fiery furnace affair (Daniel 3). The disciples may meet to celebrate the anniversary of the Last Supper, or the Resurrection, or the day of Pentecost, or maybe all three. All those martyred for their faith could meet to recount the awesome privilege of giving their lives for the Master.

I think that Heaven could host huge conventions of those who served as Sunday school teachers, choir members, or deacons. There may be massive meetings of missionaries, great gatherings of pastors, or events held for evangelists. Why won't church planters convene, worship leaders unite, and small group leaders cluster?

So What?

Knowing that Heaven will be a huge family reunion comforts me with the assurance that I will see Mom and Dad again. It humbles me with the thought of having the opportunity to thank those that helped me get on, and stay on, the path to Heaven. It also motivates me to keep helping others get there, so we can enjoy eternity together.

NOTES

1. Don Piper with Cecil B. Murphey, *90 Minutes in Heaven: A True Story of Death and Life* (Grand Rapids: Baker, 2004), 25.
2. "A Miner's Last Words," Columbus *Dispatch* (January 6, 2006), 1.
3. Piper, 21–28.

You Ain't Seen Nothin' Yet

The very first word man was ever given regarding God is that He is the Good Creator. In the beginning, God created humans and a vast variety of amazing plants and animals. His inventive genius produced an astounding array of stars and planets. He made the breathtaking beauty of the sunset. When He was finished, even He was impressed with His work and described it as "very good" (Genesis 1:1–31).

Elsewhere, scripture makes it clear that the primary player in the creation of the universe was God the Son, Jesus Christ.

> *Through him all things were made; without*
> *him nothing was made that has been made.*
>
> John 1:3

> *For by him all things were created: things*
> *in heaven and on earth, visible and invisible,*
> *whether thrones or powers or rulers or authorities;*
> *all things were created by him and for him.*
>
> Colossians 1:16

> *In these last days he has spoken to us by his*
> *Son, whom he appointed heir of all things, and*
> *through whom he made the universe.*
>
> Hebrews 1:2

When God became man (Jesus), He became a carpenter (Mark 6:3). Carpenters are creators. Good carpenters will look at a lifeless piece of wood and see something valuable and beautiful. Carefully and skillfully, they will craft it to detailed specifications. They will lovingly polish it, and when it is ready they will proudly show it to others. Creating beautiful things is what excellent carpenters do.

Jesus wanted to encourage His disciples in the wake of His nearing departure. He gave them a powerful promise that He was going to take on a massive renovation and building project—Heaven.

> *"Do not let your hearts be troubled. Trust in God; trust also in me. In my Father's house are many rooms; if it were not so, I would have told you. I am going there to prepare a place for you. And if I go and prepare a place for you, I will come back and take you to be with me that you also may be where I am."*
>
> JOHN 14:1–3

Jesus was telling them that Heaven, although perfect in its present state at that time, was not yet fully prepared. He wanted to continue modifying and expanding it to suit its coming inhabitants. This means that ever since Jesus spoke those words in the first century, Heaven has been under renovation, being remodeled, enlarged, and enhanced by the Magnificent Creator, Marvelous Carpenter, and Master Craftsman, Jesus Christ. Wow!

Heaven is a world far greater than this one, but far less than the one to come.

Change in Heaven

My family began when Cathy and I were married in 1981. Over the past twenty-five years, three boys have come into our family and much has occurred. Yet the essence of our family has not changed much. We try to put God first, be church-centered, grow as individuals, and make a difference in our world. Although our family dynamics have changed through the years as children have been added and progressed through various stages, and it will undoubtedly change in the future as daughters-in-law and grandbabies are added, it will still be our family. It is currently not all it will one day be.

Heaven is similar in that it has and will continue to undergo some changes, additions, expansions, and renovations while maintaining its core distinctive. In any of its stages, Heaven is the place of blessed reward for God's faithful children. It is God's home and man's hope. Yet much of what the Bible says about Heaven can become confusing until we understand that Heaven, as it is, is not yet all it will ultimately become.

The Phases of Heaven

Heaven past, Heaven present, and Heaven future should all be understood as Heaven, but must not be viewed as being exactly the same. The Bible describes at least five phases of heaven. Each stage is still heaven, yet is slightly different than the others.

1. Early Heaven

Early Heaven is the Heaven that existed until the time Satan led a mutiny against God (Isaiah 14:12–15; Ezekiel 28:12–17). Joining Satan were up to a third of the angels (Revelation 12:4, 9). This is nearly all we know about Early Heaven. Was there a stage of Heaven prior to this? We don't know.

2. Abraham's Side

After the fall of Satan and prior to the resurrection of Jesus, Heaven was one side of two compartments of one place called "Sheol" in Hebrew, or "Hades" in Greek. The two compartments were divided by an uncrossable chasm (Luke 16:26). Jesus called the heavenly side "Abraham's side" (Luke 16:22). The other compartment was an earlier version of Hell (Luke 16:23). Those on Abraham's side experienced the pleasure of God's presence (Psalm 16:11). Those on the other side were in misery (Luke 16:23).

3. Paradise or the Third Heaven

On the cross, Jesus promised the repentant thief that he would soon join Jesus in "paradise" (Luke 23:43). Seemingly, Jesus was planning on relocating the heavenly compartment of Sheol. The scriptures teach that Paradise is where believers now ascend directly into the Lord's presence at the time of physical death (Ephesians 4:8–10; 2 Corinthians 5:8). It is the place to which Jesus ascended in a cloud and the place from which He will one day return.

> *After he said this, he was taken up before their very eyes, and a cloud hid him from their sight. They were looking intently up into the sky as he was going, when suddenly two men dressed in white stood beside them. "Men of Galilee," they said, "why do you stand here looking into the sky? This same Jesus, who has been taken from you into heaven, will come back in the same way you have seen him go into heaven."*
>
> ACTS 1:9–11

Paradise is the "far better" place Paul was privileged to see and, thereafter, longed for. He called it "the third heaven" (2 Corinthians 12:1–4). The first heaven is the domain of birds and clouds, the second heaven is what we call outer space. For Paul, being in Paradise was "gain" (i.e., "more life") compared to life on earth, primarily because Christ is there (Philippians 1:21–23).

> *For to me, to live is Christ and to die is gain. If I am to go on living in the body, this will mean fruitful labor for me. Yet what shall I choose? I do not know! I am torn between the two: I desire to depart and be with Christ, which is better by far.*
>
> PHILIPPIANS 1:21–23

> *I must go on boasting. Although there is nothing to be gained, I will go on to visions and revelations from the Lord. I know a man in Christ who fourteen years ago was caught up to the third heaven. . .[he] was caught up to paradise.*
>
> 2 CORINTHIANS 12:1– 2, 4

John also was honored to see visions of Paradise (Revelation 2:7). Fortunately, he was encouraged to write down what he saw (Revelation 1:19). And we are deeply indebted to John for much of our knowledge about Heaven.

Paradise is the present stage of Heaven. It is the heavenly place my mom and dad now call home. Every believer who has died since Jesus' resurrection has gone directly to Paradise. Paradise is where I am confidently preparing to go when I die.

It is the place where I hope to meet you face to face.

Some believe Paradise exists as a different dimension alongside our visible universe. Others feel it may be a distinct universe with portals to ours. We don't know for sure. We do know that this present realm of Paradise is an angelic realm. It is distinct from the earth. Except in rare, isolated incidents, it is invisible to our current human eyes. It is a spiritual dimension with physical elements. Occasionally people could see into it or see beings from Paradise (Acts 7:55–59; 2 Kings 6:17). People in it have or assume some sort of visible bodies (Matthew 17:3).

Paradise will undergo a transition of its own during the time of Tribulation on Earth. The amazing prophetic books of Daniel and Revelation and some of Jesus' final teachings tell us much about the future happenings on planet Earth. After a departure of the Christians in an event known as the Rapture, Earth will experience seven dreadful years of pain and suffering known as the Tribulation. The Antichrist will assume a season of power and will use it to persecute and execute many of God's people. Great numbers of Jewish people will return to faith in Jesus as their Messiah. At the end of these seven years of tribulation, King Jesus will return to Earth to establish His kingdom.

While the Bible is clear about many earthly events and even much of the timing of these events during the seven years of the Tribulation, it is not as specific about the timing of the happenings in Heaven during this time. As I link the pieces of the puzzle together, I see several major events that believers in Heaven will experience as they transition from Paradise to the millennial Kingdom. These include the resurrection of the dead and rapture of the living (1 Thessalonians 4:13–18), the judgment seat of Christ (2 Corinthians 5:10), and the wedding supper of the Lamb (Revelation 19:6–9).

4. The Millennial Kingdom

The Bible describes a glorious time when Jesus Christ will return to reign as King on Earth for one thousand years (Revelation 20:1–10). There is much we do not currently understand about the millennial Kingdom. However, we do know that Jesus will bring a season of tremendous tranquility to this planet. This will be an unprecedented, glorious time of prosperity and peace on Earth.

> *"The wolf and the lamb will feed together,*
> *and the lion will eat straw like the ox, but dust*
> *will be the serpent's food. They will neither harm*
> *nor destroy on all my holy mountain," says the*
> *LORD.*
>
> ISAIAH 65:25

5. The New Heaven and the New Earth

Heaven is not yet all it will be. When John saw into the future, he saw "a *new* heaven and a *new* earth" (Revelation 21:1, emphasis added). Following the millennial Kingdom, sin, suffering, and sorrow will be completely removed from this earth. Earth will be reborn, resurrected, and remade into something wonderfully new, and even better than paradise is right now.

> *Then I saw a new heaven and a new earth. . . .*
> *And I heard a loud voice from the throne saying,*
> *"Now the dwelling of God is with men, and he*
> *will live with them. They will be his people, and*
> *God himself will be with them and be their God.*
> *He will wipe every tear from their eyes. There*
> *will be no more death or mourning or crying or*
> *pain, for the old order of things has passed away."*

He who was seated on the throne said, "I am making everything new!"

REVELATION 21:1, 3–5

Many view the new Heaven and new Earth of Revelation 21 and 22 as Heaven the way it ultimately will be. This may or may not be the case. There may be further phases of Heaven following this one; the Bible does not say. Since Heaven is an eternal place, I would not be surprised if the Master Builder continued to renovate Heaven, each phase being yet more glorious than the one before.

So What?

The size, scope, quality, beauty, functionality, and value of any construction project are limited by its location and the skills, resources, and imagination of its designer and builder. Remember, the designer and builder of Heaven is our unlimited God. Although we do not currently know all there is to know about it, we do know the One who created the wonders we call our universe has been working on preparing Heaven for nearly two thousand years. Therefore, it will be truly amazing and will only get better.

Paradise, Heaven

My friend and writing mentor, Norm Rohrer, grew up in Paradise. . .that's Paradise, Pennsylvania. Paradise, PA, is a beautiful little town tucked in the heart of Pennsylvania Dutch country in Lancaster County. This picturesque place is known for peaceful living, rich fruit farms, and the nationally acclaimed cornfield maze, "The Amazing Maize Maze."

Norm tells me that it was a great place to grow up. He says that he smiles when he thinks of Heaven, because if Paradise, Pennsylvania, was such a fantastic hometown, then how much *more* wonderful life will be in *the* Paradise we call Heaven. In other words, as great as it is, Paradise, Pennsylvania, will not compare to Paradise, Heaven.

Paradise, Heaven

Since my mom and dad have already departed from Earth and taken the trip to Paradise, Heaven, I often wonder what Paradise must be like and what their lives are like now. A quick look at the Bible tells me the word "paradise" is found three times. By looking up those verses I discover that my parents, like the thief Jesus comforted on the cross, are with the Lord in Paradise (Luke 23:43; 2 Corinthians 5:8). I find that Paul saw a glimpse of Paradise and deeply desired to return there as opposed to staying on Earth (2 Corinthians 12:1–4; Philippians 1:21–23). Based on Paul's words, I believe my parents are definitely somewhere more desirable than Earth.

I also notice that in John's revelation, Jesus told him that spiritual overcomers would eat from the tree of life found in Paradise (Revelation 2:7). Therefore, Mom and Dad must now be in a literal place graced by access to the extremely powerful tree of life.

But what is life like in Paradise? The Bible gives us many clues.

Clues from the Garden of Eden

The word "Paradise" comes from an Iranian word meaning "enclosed park or garden."[1] It also is used to refer to the Garden of Eden in the Greek version of the Old Testament (Genesis 2:8; Ezekiel 28:13). This makes sense, as it will be the domain of the tree of life that adorned the original Garden of Eden (Revelation 2:7; Genesis 3:24). Ancient Jews felt that Heaven was a restored Eden. The best way to understand Heaven as it is today is to think of it as a restored and perfected Garden of Eden.

Paradise, Heaven, is a restored, purified, and perfected Garden of Eden.

God called Eden "very good" (Genesis 1:31). In Eden, Adam and Eve had brand-new bodies that had the appearance of age and maturity (they were man and woman, not newborns). The garden was filled with fantastic fruit trees (2:9). Rivers flowed through the garden (2:10–14). Adam was given the responsibility of working and protecting the garden (2:15). Humans had a good relationship with the animals (2:19–20). Adam and Eve were married in Eden (2:24). They lived in innocence (2:25). They communicated with each other (3:6), with at least some of the animals (3:1–2), and directly with God (3:9–10).

So I assume that, quite possibly, Paradise, Heaven, is quite similar to what the Garden of Eden was before sin. Like Eden, it is an extremely pleasant garden, carefully cultivated, lush, and filled with gorgeous exotic plants and animals. Paradise is totally free of any form of pollution, contamination, corruption, perversion, and sin. It is a place of boundless beauty, profound rest, and tremendous tranquility. God Himself walks there and is accessible for conversations. No wonder it's called Heaven!

The residents in Paradise will probably have wonderful, prime bodies; amazing and healthy meals; and meaningful work. Like the Garden of Eden, there are animals, and Mom and Dad may be able to talk with them! No doubt they are waiting for the ultimate and perfect union with Christ at the marriage supper of the Lamb. They are undoubtedly enjoying an incredibly delightful time in a wonderfully pleasant place.

Clues from the Mount of Transfiguration

There are a couple of men who were permanently relocated to Heaven, yet returned to Earth briefly. Their names are Moses and Elijah. Observing how they were described can give us some clue as to what people are like in Paradise right now.

> *Jesus. . .took Peter, John and James with him and went up onto a mountain to pray. As he was praying, the appearance of his face changed, and his clothes became as bright as a flash of lightning. Two men, Moses and Elijah, appeared in glorious splendor, talking with Jesus. They spoke about his departure, which he was about to bring to fulfillment at Jerusalem. Peter and his companions . . .saw his glory and the two men standing with him.*

> LUKE 9:28–32

The above passage about Moses and Elijah tells us several important facts about people in Paradise. First, they were recognizable for who they really were. Peter and John had never seen them before but immediately knew their names and identities. Second, they had some sort of perceivable, physical bodies. Third, the bodies they had carried a remarkable, incandescent radiance. This splendor either came from the bodies themselves or was reflected glory from the place they had recently departed, Paradise. Fourth, they were able to speak with one another. Fifth, they spoke with Jesus face to face. Sixth, they were aware of what was happening with Jesus on Earth. Seventh, they had some knowledge of the future as it was about to unfold in the life of Jesus.

From this account, I assume Mom and Dad will be immediately recognizable to themselves and others. They have some sort of nifty radiant bodies. They can talk to each other and others. They can talk to Jesus! They probably have some idea of what is happening on Earth involving events relating to God's Kingdom. They may even have some knowledge of other events, like what is occurring in the lives of their children and grandchildren. They also may have a good understanding of what is about to happen in the future.

Clues from Lazarus the Beggar

Jesus told a fascinating story about a rich man who went to Hell and a beggar named Lazarus who inhabited an early phase of Heaven. As previously stated, after the fall of Satan and prior to the resurrection of Jesus, Heaven was one of two compartments of what was referred to as "Sheol" in Hebrew. Jesus called the heavenly side "Abraham's side" (Luke 16:22). The other compartment is an earlier version of Hell (Luke 16:23). The bulk of this story is about the man in Hell. We can conclude that much of what was true of Lazarus in Abraham's side will be true of people in the updated version of Heaven, called Paradise.

"There was a rich man who was dressed
in purple and fine linen and lived in luxury
every day. At his gate was laid a beggar named

*Lazarus. . . . The time came when the beggar
died and the angels carried him to Abraham's
side. The rich man also died and was buried. In
hell, where he was in torment, he looked up and
saw Abraham far away, with Lazarus by his side.
So he called to him, 'Father Abraham, have pity
on me and send Lazarus to dip the tip of his finger in water and cool my tongue, because I am in
agony in this fire.'"*

LUKE 16:19, 22–24

In Jesus' story, Lazarus was carried to Heaven by angels. This is also probably what happens to Christians who die today. Lazarus was recognizable, just as Elijah and Moses were recognizable. People in Paradise won't be shapeless, formless, ethereal ghosts.

*"But Abraham replied, 'Son, remember that
in your lifetime you received your good things,
while Lazarus received bad things, but now he is
comforted here and you are in agony. And besides
all this, between us and you a great chasm has
been fixed, so that those who want to go from
here to you cannot, nor can anyone cross over
from there to us.'"*

LUKE 16:25–26

Lazarus was receiving comfort in Heaven. My parents both suffered at the end of their earthly lives. It is encouraging to know that they are now in a place of comfort. Lazarus's destiny was fixed. My parents both loved God. It is good to know that their place in Paradise is secure.

> *"He answered, 'Then I beg you, father, send*
> *Lazarus to my father's house, for I have five*
> *brothers. Let him warn them, so that they will*
> *not also come to this place of torment.' Abraham*
> *replied, 'They have Moses and the Prophets; let*
> *them listen to them.' 'No, father Abraham,' he*
> *said, 'but if someone from the dead goes to them,*
> *they will repent.' He said to him, 'If they do not*
> *listen to Moses and the Prophets, they will not be*
> *convinced even if someone rises from the dead.'"*

> LUKE 16:27–31

Lazarus was not allowed to leave Heaven to intervene in the affairs of people on Earth. They were to work on their own destinies based on the guidance of the scriptures. I assume this is also true of my parents and others in Paradise. They may see what we are experiencing, but they probably are not permitted to interfere with it.

Other Clues

There are a few other scriptures that shed light on the goings-on in Paradise. Although these scriptures are not conclusive, they leave some interesting clues.

> *Therefore, since we are surrounded by such*
> *a great cloud of witnesses, let us throw off every-*
> *thing that hinders and the sin that so easily*
> *entangles, and let us run with perseverance the*
> *race marked out for us.*

> HEBREWS 12:1

Scholars debate the identity of these witnesses who surround us, but it is entirely possible that the believers in Paradise somehow can see our efforts to follow God and cheer us on.

In Luke chapter 15, Jesus tells the stories of the lost sheep, the lost coin and the lost son. In each case the result of the successful pursuit was a joyous party. What is interesting is that He also says that a party is thrown in Heaven when a sinner repents.

> *"I tell you that in the same way there will be more rejoicing in heaven over one sinner who repents than over ninety-nine righteous persons who do not need to repent."*
>
> LUKE 15:7

It is probable that the ones described as "rejoicing" in this verse are not only the members of the holy Trinity or just the holy angels. Friends and relatives, pastors and missionaries will also join in the joyous occasion. People on the other side understand the supreme significance of salvation more deeply than we do (Luke 16:27–28). It only makes sense that one of the greatest sources of delight and happiness for believers in Heaven will be to observe the marvelous miracle of regeneration in the lives of those with whom they have shared and love.

The apostle Peter makes an offhand but extremely insightful comment about God's relationship to time in his last letter.

> *But do not forget this one thing, dear friends: With the Lord a day is like a thousand years, and a thousand years are like a day.*
>
> 2 PETER 3:8

Peter's point is that God lives outside of the realm of time. I assume that once we leave our earthly lives and enter Paradise we also will enter a world that operates largely outside the realm of time. Time will have no meaning in Heaven as it does on Earth.

So What?

Based on what we have studied about Paradise, we can conclude that Paradise, Heaven, is not totally unlike Earth at its very best. It is simply much, much better. It is like a restored, purified, and perfected Garden of Eden.

Writing this chapter has given me peace. Instead of wondering if my parents are some sort of mystical, disembodied spirits, I can picture my parents younger, stronger, and more vibrant then ever, but still themselves—their very best selves. They live in the most delightful, wonderful, lovely place ever created or imagined. Harmony and deep happiness rule the day. They are living in a place of vibrant rest. And they are communing with God.

I am also reminded of the incredible importance of inspiring others to put their faith in Jesus Christ as their Savior. Their eventual turning to God will bring great joy to untold others in Paradise.

NOTES

1. *Webster's Ninth Collegiate Dictionary* (Springfield MA: Merriman-Webster Inc. Publishers, 1987), 853.

9

HEAVEN'S AWARDS BANQUET

I'll never forget my first real awards banquet. It was early evening in the spring of my sophomore year. We wore suits and our parents joined us for the Winter Sports Awards Banquet. The cafeteria of Chillicothe High School was the same as usual, except for two things: the walls were decorated with blue and white streamers, and sitting on a long table was a stunning array of big blue and silver trophies.

Excitedly, we chewed the mandatory rubbery chicken dinner with the artificial mashed potatoes, plastic-tasting green beans, and white rolls. After we washed down the stale cake with a couple of glasses of overly sweetened iced tea, the school officials began to honor the athletes of the various teams. I quickly noticed that the athletes fit into three categories and received three types of awards based on their category.

First were the people who had made the team. They received a paper certificate for being on the team. Every athlete got one of those. No negative comments were made about any of the team members. Everything shared that night was the positive observation of the person's performance and effort.

Next to be honored were the varsity athletes who had played on the varsity team. Those select individuals got big, fluffy, white letter *C*s with blue trim. They were the lettermen. I was pretty excited because I was earning a varsity letter as a sophomore.

But it was the last, select group that caught my attention. They were given the few big, beautiful silver trophies. They were the top varsity athletes, who got trophies for leading the team in scoring, being the most dedicated, or being the most valuable. They were the ones selected all-league, all-district, or even all-state.

Several years later I was reading in my Bible about the great awards banquet that will be attended by everyone who goes to Heaven. I had come to understand that at the judgment seat of Christ we would be rewarded for the sacrifice and the sweat we had put forth for God down here on Earth. I was impressed by how similar and also by how much different, more important, and better the heavenly awards presentation would be, compared to the Winter Sports Banquet at Chillicothe High School.

At the heavenly awards banquet, only those who are on Jesus' "team" by faith in Christ as Savior will be invited. Everyone on the team will be recognized. No negative comments will made about any of the team members. Everything shared will be the positive observation of the person's performance and effort spent serving Christ. Some will receive special recognition for their extra efforts and achievements by receiving crowns, commendations, and commissions.

Heaven will be the site of a wonderful awards banquet.

Judgment Day

> *Just as man is destined to die once, and after that to face judgment.*

> HEBREWS 9:27

The Bible does not teach reincarnation. After death, we face judgment. This begins as a judgment of faith. Those who have placed their faith in Jesus Christ are ushered immediately into Paradise. Those without faith in Christ are not. Those with names recorded in the Lamb's book of life are escorted to Paradise. Those whose names have not been written there face an eternity without God.

Sometime subsequent to death everyone will face a second judgment. This judgment is focused on how they have lived and what they have done. Nonfollowers of Jesus Christ will face the terrifying great white throne judgment (Revelation 20:11–13). However, followers of Christ attend the tremendously encouraging judgment seat of Christ.

Judgment Seat of Christ	*Great White Throne of Judgment*
2 Corinthians 5:10	Revelation 20:11–13
Believers only	Non-Christians
Awards Banquet	Courtroom
Rewards given	Punishment doled out
Positive	Negative

The judgment seat of Christ is an awards ceremony. The great white throne judgment is a courtroom. The judgment seat of Christ is a positive event we should prepare for and anticipate. The great white throne judgment must be avoided and can be, by placing your faith in Jesus Christ's death, burial, and resurrection for your sins.

Not an Entrance Exam

Contrary to many very funny jokes, Saint Peter is not at the gates of Heaven with a clipboard, checking off those who get in and those who don't based on the judgment seat of Christ. That will already have been decided. Everyone at the judgment seat of Christ will be a follower of Jesus. They are the ones already on His team through faith. Everyone being evaluated will be already in Heaven.

The judgment seat of Christ will not be a place of punishing people for poor performance. No punishment is given out, only rewards. If you are a true Christian, the Bible states very clearly, "There is therefore now *no condemnation* for those who are in Christ Jesus" (Romans 8:1 NASB, emphasis added).

Jesus took all the punishment for our sins when He died on the cross. He didn't just die for *some* of our sins. He died to pay for *all* of our sins. His sacrifice was sufficient to cover the full debt of our sins. Note Hebrews 8:12 (NKJV), which states, "For I will be merciful to their unrighteousness, and *their sins and their lawless deeds I will remember no more*"(emphasis added). When we are saved, our sins are forgiven and functionally forgotten by God forever! There will be no punishment for sins handed out at the judgment seat of Christ. It is the heavenly awards banquet.

The Heavenly Awards Stand

> *For we must all appear before the judgment seat of Christ, that each one may receive the things done in the body, according to what he has done, whether good or bad.*
>
> 2 CORINTHIANS 5:10 NKJV

When you read the words "judgment seat," do not think courtroom; rather think of an awards stand. To us the concept of judgment sounds rather negative, but this is an unquestionably positive event. In the first century BC, in the city of Corinth, there were some games that were actually more popular than the Olympic games held in Athens. They were called the Isthmian games and were held every two years in the Greek city. In these games, the winner of each event would be led in front of the judge's stand where the judge, usually the highest dignitary in attendance (the mayor or the governor), would put a laurel crown on the victor's head.

The concept of the judgment seat of Christ is not so much a judicial one as an athletic one. Don't picture a courtroom—picture an Olympic stadium, an awards stand, or, even better, an awards banquet. Don't think of punishment being doled out by a judge—instead, picture awards given out by the greatest dignitary and head coach of them all—the King of kings, the Lord of lords, Jesus Christ.

> *"And behold, I am coming quickly, and My reward is with Me, to give to every one according to his work."*
>
> REVELATION 22:12 NKJV

Judge Jesus

When we are evaluated at the judgment seat of Christ, who will evaluate us? The scripture says, "For we must all appear before the judgment seat of *Christ*" (2 Corinthians 5:10 NKJV, emphasis added). This is also seen in John 5:22 (NKJV): "For the Father judges no one, but has committed all judgment to *the Son*" (emphasis added). Speaking of Jesus, the apostle Peter said, "He is the one whom God appointed as judge of the living and the dead" (Acts 10:42). The apostle Paul said in 2 Timothy 4:8 (NKJV), "Finally, there is laid up for me the crown of righteousness, which *the Lord, the righteous Judge*, will give to me on that Day, and not to me only but also to all who have loved His appearing" (emphasis added).

A perfect evaluator should know all the facts, be just and righteous, and have empathy for the one evaluated. Jesus is the perfect evaluator-judge. As the Son of God, He knows absolutely every detail about you. He also is perfectly just and righteous. Beyond that, two thousand years ago He stepped down out of Heaven and came to Earth, not as a spectator of human life, but as a full participant. Jesus was born in a barn. He had to learn to walk and talk. He was a teenager. He was tempted. He had friends and enemies. He got hungry, thirsty, and tired. He died. Therefore, He can fully empathize with everything we have gone through, making Him the perfect judge (Hebrews 2:14–18).

Some people find the thought of this detailed examination a little unnerving. If you are the type of person who puts on a good front but has some nasty secrets, let me remind you Jesus knows those secrets, and He is not fooled. Now is the time to make whatever adjustments are necessary.

However, there is also great comfort in the fact that Jesus is our only judge. People's evaluations of us can be inaccurate. Jesus won't make any mistake, and He won't miss any of the good we have done, even if no one else takes notice. Ultimately, there is only one person we have to please: our judge, the Lord Jesus.

Refined by Fire

When the apostle John saw the resurrected Jesus in Heaven, he was deeply impressed that Jesus' eyes were like flames of fire (Revelation 1:14). Fire is a powerful purifier. It is used to burn the impurities out of precious metals. Heaven is a perfect place, and before we fully enter into it, our lives down here on Earth will need to be purified and refined. Paul described the judgment seat of Christ as an examination by fire.

> *For no other foundation can anyone lay than*
> *that which is laid, which is Jesus Christ. Now*
> *if anyone builds on this foundation with gold,*
> *silver, precious stones, wood, hay, straw, each one's*
> *work will become clear; for the Day will declare*
> *it, because it will be revealed by fire; and the fire*
> *will test each one's work, of what sort it is. If any-*
> *one's work which he has built on it endures, he*
> *will receive a reward. If anyone's work is burned,*
> *he will suffer loss; but he himself will be saved,*
> *yet so as through fire.*

I CORINTHIANS 3:11–15 NKJV

Jesus, the Evaluator, will examine our lives. As His eyes of fire see the positives, described here as gold, silver, or precious stones, they will be refined and made more evident, more beautiful. The negatives, described as wood, hay, or straw, will be burned up. The good works we have done in our lives will be refined and rewarded. Based on how we lived and what we did for God down on Earth, we will receive rewards such as crowns, commendations, and commissions.

Casting Crowns

The purpose of winning crowns is not selfish. In fact it is the exact opposite. The purpose of winning crowns is to have as many as possible to cast at Jesus' feet (Revelation 4:9–11). This will be our way of telling Him "thank you" for all He has done for us.

Temporary Trophy

After attending the awards banquet my sophomore year in high school, I decided I'd go all out to win a trophy my next year. Every day for the next year, I made sacrifices in order to achieve my goal. I worked out more often, lifted more weights, and ran more miles. I lived on a Spartan diet. It paid off. In fact, one year later, I earned the Most Valuable Player award for my team.

A couple of years after that, I was home from college. I looked at my MVP trophy and found that my nameplate had fallen off. Then it hit me: Earthly trophies won't last, but heavenly trophies will last forever.

So What?

Heaven will have an awesome awards banquet where we can receive eternal rewards; but first, we need to be certain that we will be there by making sure we are on the team. If you have not done so already, you can join this team by making Jesus your personal Lord and Savior. Second, we all need to earn our "varsity letter" by not just coasting, but fully engaging in His service. Third, we must start living for eternity and go all out to win trophies that we can give back to Jesus.

10

Prepare Yourself

I have a recurring dream—well, actually it's more of a nightmare. I bet many of you have had it as well. The essence of the dream is this: It is the day of final exams. I am walking through my high school on my way to take a final exam. As I am scurrying down the hall, terror is slowly rising in my heart, as I realize that I have not prepared for this final. I have not studied. I have not even read the books that were assigned.

I begin to sweat when I realize it has been weeks since I even attended the class. In fact, my attendance was so infrequent I am not sure where the room is. Terror takes over. Frantically, I dash around unfamiliar hallways. Time is running out and I not only don't have time to prepare, I can't even find the room to take the test. I am engulfed in dread knowing I am completely unprepared. Just as I think things could not get any worse, I look down and notice. . .that I am not wearing pants!

Prepare Yourself!

Having two sons in college and being a college professor, I find some enjoyment in the following tale about a college freshman who really enjoyed his first semester away from Mom and Dad. In fact, he enjoyed it so much, he hadn't done any studying. Just prior to Parents' Weekend, he e-mailed his mom:

Having a great time.
Send money.
Flunking all my classes.
Prepare Pop.

Mom emailed back:

Pop prepared.
Prepare yourself!

The most life-changing truth about Heaven is that life on Earth is merely the preparation for eternity in Heaven. We can increase our capacity to enjoy Heaven tomorrow by the choices we make today. The eternal investments we make now will determine where we start there.

You can increase your capacity to enjoy Heaven tomorrow by the choices you make today.

Two thousand years ago, God gave the warning "man is destined to die once, and after that to face examination" (Hebrews 9:27, author's paraphrase). At the heavenly awards banquet, we will undergo the most comprehensive final exam ever administered. Theologians call this exam the judgment seat of Christ. He will evaluate us, looking to reward everything He can in our lives. We will be given crowns, commendations, and commissions as awards. There will be so much to experience and enjoy in Heaven. How we live on earth will directly influence our capacity to fully take pleasure in Heaven.

A study of the Bible reveals many areas of life that the Lord will evaluate. I found the top nine areas of evaluation that you and I need to be prepared for on that day of our final exam. We need to get out our syllabus, the Bible, to see what is coming and to start getting ready for it now.

The Top Areas of Examination

1. Our Motives, Thoughts, and Deeds

> *"I, the LORD, search the heart, I test the*
> *mind, even to give every man according to his*
> *ways, according to the fruit of his doings."*
> JEREMIAH 17:10 NKJV

The Lord will examine us from the inside out. This will include our affections, our thoughts, and our deeds since becoming a Christian. Every selfless, unnoticed act we have ever done will be rewarded. Our private thoughts of God will be recognized.

2. Our Words

> *"But I say to you that for every idle word*
> *men may speak, they will give account of it in the*
> *day of judgment."*
> MATTHEW 12:36 NKJV

The verse is quite clear. The Lord will examine our words. Every time we shared Jesus with a coworker, prayed for someone else, or uttered words of praise to God, Jesus will acknowledge and reward it. However, our ungodly, unwholesome, unkind words will be burned up.

3. Our Treatment of Others

> *For God is not unjust to forget your work and*
> *labor of love which you have shown toward His*
> *name, in that you have ministered to the saints,*
> *and do minister.*
> HEBREWS 6:10 NKJV

> *"He who receives a prophet in the name of*
> *a prophet shall receive a prophet's reward. And*
> *he who receives a righteous man in the name of*
> *a righteous man shall receive a righteous man's*
> *reward. And whoever gives one of these little ones*
> *only a cup of cold water in the name of a dis-*
> *ciple, assuredly, I say to you, he shall by no means*
> *lose his reward."*
>
> MATTHEW 10:41–42 NKJV

> *"And whoever welcomes a little child like this*
> *in my name welcomes me."*
>
> MATTHEW 18:5

These verses point out that God is very concerned with the way we treat others. Sometimes I forget that the Lord may have put that needy person or that difficult person in my life on purpose. He is giving me a chance to show them love and serve them, in part, so He can give me a reward. Sometimes I forget that the way I view and treat others is, in one way, a microcosm of how I view the Lord.

4. Our Use of and/or Response to Spiritual Authority

> *Obey those who rule over you, and be sub-*
> *missive, for they watch out for your souls, as those*
> *who must give account. Let them do so with joy*
> *and not with grief, for that would be unprofit-*
> *able for you.*
>
> HEBREWS 13:17 NKJV

This verse tells us to watch how we respond to the spiritual authorities in our lives, because they must give an account for our souls. The context here is talking about pastors. But I believe the principle applies in a broader sense. I will give an account of how I acted not merely as a pastor, but also as a husband, a father, and an employer. Also, I think that if persons in authority are accountable for how they use it, those under authority will also be accountable for how they respond to spiritual authority. How did they treat a father, husband, pastor, or church leader?

5. Our Evangelistic Efforts

> *For what is our hope, our joy, or the crown in which we will glory in the presence of our Lord Jesus when he comes? Is it not you? Indeed, you are our glory and joy.*

1 THESSALONIANS 2:19

Everybody we help get to Heaven will become a crown for us. They may be in Heaven as a result of our inviting them to church, sharing our testimony, praying for them, or giving to outreach projects. I anticipate being warmly welcomed into Heaven by everyone I helped to get there. The joy in their faces will be an incredible reward for whatever role I had in their decision to trust Christ.

6. Our Use of Money

Jesus talked about giving an account of how we use our money more than any other topic. He mentioned it in about half of the parables He told. He knew there is often no clearer picture of our spiritual condition than how we handle and give our money. Paul built on the teachings of Jesus when he wrote,

> *Command those who are rich in this present age not to be haughty, nor to trust in uncertain riches but in the living God, who gives us richly all things to enjoy. Let them do good, that they be rich in good works, ready to give, willing to share, storing up for themselves a good foundation for the time to come, that they may lay hold on eternal life.*
>
> 1 TIMOTHY 6:17–19 NKJV
>
> (SEE ALSO MATTHEW 25:14–23, LUKE 12:21; 16:9–14)

7. Our Willingness to Suffer for Christ

> *"Blessed are you when they revile and persecute you, and say all kinds of evil against you falsely for My sake. Rejoice and be exceedingly glad, for great is your reward in heaven, for so they persecuted the prophets who were before you."*
>
> MATTHEW 5:11–12 NKJV

> *"Do not be afraid of what you are about to suffer. I tell you, the devil will put some of you in prison to test you, and you will suffer persecution for ten days. Be faithful, even to the point of death, and I will give you the crown of life."*
>
> REVELATION 2:10

There are many thousands of faithful Christians in other parts of the world who truly suffer for their faith. Many even die for Jesus. I am so happy that on the day of evaluation they will be recognized and richly rewarded for their sufferings and sacrifices. They will be receiving "most valuable" awards and lengthy standing ovations.

8. Our Service

One of the chief reasons for the judgment seat is to reward our service for Jesus Christ. The New Testament simply assumes that every Christian will actively serve Christ. When you find a place of service in your church, you are preparing for the coming of Jesus. He desires every member to minister. Whether your place is setting up the chairs on Saturday, working in the nursery, working the lights, teaching a Sunday school class, helping get cars parked, greeting people on their way in, leading a small group, working with teenagers, or singing in the choir, every member needs to be a minister.

The Bible gives several significant criteria with which Jesus will evaluate our service.

The Criteria for Evaluating Our Works

1. Content: Good or bad? Worthwhile or worthless? 2 Corinthians 5:10
2. Motive: To please people or God? Matthew 6:1
3. Source: His strength or ours? John 15:5
4. Faithfulness: Convenient or costly? 1 Corinthians 4:2
5. Quality: Heavenly or earthly? Matthew 6:19–20
6. Proportion: All-out or partial? Luke 12:48

9. Our Level of Church Participation

Let us not give up meeting together, as some are in the habit of doing, but let us encourage one another—and all the more as you see the Day approaching.

HEBREWS 10:25

The author of Hebrews wrote to people who were experiencing persecution because of their church involvement. As a result of the persecution, some wanted to stop drawing attention to themselves and had stopped worshiping together. He encouraged them to "go to church!"

I doubt that many of us miss church because we are trying to avoid persecution. Some people think they can be good Christians but not be involved in a church. The New Testament does not assume that anyone can be a Christian without being actively involved in a local church. It is a nonnegotiable. God will evaluate your level of involvement in His beloved institution—the church.

So What?

For me, the difference between high school and college was the difference between night and day. Of course, college was much harder and had much more homework than high school. But interestingly, I got much better grades in college than in high school.

Did I get smarter in college? No and yes. No, my IQ did not go up. Yes, I got smarter, in that I always made sure I was prepared. In high school I tried to cram and it was never enough. My grades showed it.

In college I started preparing for my finals the first day of class and almost every day in between. On a few occasions, I got some of the highest grades my professors had given. The tests were not something I dreaded; I actually enjoyed them because I was well prepared. I also learned and retained much more than I had in high school.

Shortly after arriving in Heaven, you will be taking your final exam. How you do on your exam will determine how much you will enjoy Heaven. You have all you need in order to be prepared because you have a syllabus, the Bible. So prepare yourself.

TOTAL BODY MAKEOVER

11

> *The body of B. Franklin, printer,*
> *(Like the Cover of an Old Book,*
> *Its Contents torn Out*
> *And Stript of its Lettering and Gilding)*
> *Lies Here, Food for Worms.*
> *But the Work shall not be Lost;*
> *For it will (as he Believ'd) Appear once More*
> *In a New and More Elegant edition,*
> *Revised and Corrected*
> *By the Author.*
>
> FRANKLIN'S SELF-WRITTEN EPITAPH

Every year at the end of winter, downtown Columbus, Ohio, is the home of the Arnold Sports Festival. Over a three-day period thirty events are held, including fifteen Olympic sports. Everything from arm wrestling, to weightlifting, to figure skating, to volleyball, to archery, to martial arts, to gymnastics is contested. The main events, however, are the bodybuilding competitions for men and women. Considered the most lucrative competition in bodybuilding, winners may leave with such prizes as one hundred thousand dollars cash, a huge Hummer vehicle, or a Rolex watch. The event is billed as the ultimate celebration of the human body.

I must admit that I fail to see the big appeal of bronzed,

bulging, super-sized, steroid-enhanced, chiseled muscles. The winners have obviously worked extremely hard to gain such muscle size and sculpture, but I just don't get it. So much time, expense, and energy spent building up a body that will age, sag, bag, and wear out in just a few decades.

Total Body Makeover

What I do want is a total body makeover, and I don't mean just losing some weight. I mean getting a whole new body—one that will last.

Please, don't get me wrong. I am very thankful for my body. I don't know where I'd be without it. I try to be a good steward of my body through careful diet, wise rest, and regular exercise. But it wouldn't upset me one tiny bit to trade it in on an entirely brand new model. My old version has over four decades of scars, breaks, and cavities. Frankly, "it ain't what it used to be," and for that matter, "it ain't never been all it could be." A much faster, stronger, sleeker, tanner, more attractive model would be just fine with me. One with keener eyesight and thicker hair would be nice. It would also help my basketball game if I was several inches taller.

No total body makeover on this side of eternity will last very long. Eventually, the strain of living on a sin-cursed planet wears our bodies out. One day, however, we will be given a new, improved version of our body, designed especially for eternity, honed for Heaven.

In Heaven we will get a total body makeover.

One of the best deals about Heaven is that at the resurrection of the redeemed, we will get amazing new bodies. When Jesus rose from the dead, He not only proved His deity and secured our salvation, He also guaranteed our resurrection (1 Corinthians 15:14–20). These better bodies will be issued on that "Great Gettin' Up Morning."

"Oh, That Great Gettin' Up Morning"

Pastor and writer Tony Campolo tells the story of an African-American pastor preaching a funeral sermon for a man named Clarence. After a glowing eulogy of some twenty minutes, the pastor concluded, "That's it, Clarence. There is nothing else to say. So if there is nothing else to say, I'm going to say this—'Good night!' "

Closing the lid of the casket, the preacher turned to the congregation and boomed, "And I know that God is going to give him a good morning!"

On cue the choir rose to sing, "Oh, That Great Gettin' Up Morning, We Shall Rise, We Shall Rise." Everyone jumped to their feet, clapping and singing, anticipating the glories of their resurrection.[1]

Resurrection Bodies

God gave the apostle Paul special insight into the type of bodies we would have at our resurrection. In the fifteenth chapter of his letter to the Corinthians, he described several aspects of our new bodies.

1. Perfected

Our new bodies will be perfected versions of the bodies we now have. We know from the apostle John that others will be able to recognize us (John 21:4–7). Sexual identities will remain. Racial identities will continue (Revelation 5:9; 7:9). You will still be yourself, but only much improved.

In speaking of the nature of our resurrection bodies, Paul argues that just as a seed is a precursor and smaller indication of the plant to follow, our earthly bodies are unfulfilled versions of the bodies we will receive at the resurrection. Our new bodies will be completed editions of the bodies we now wear.

> *But someone may ask, . . ."With what kind*
> *of body will they come?" How foolish! What you*
> *sow does not come to life unless it dies. When you*
> *sow, you do not plant the body that will be, but*
> *just a seed, perhaps of wheat or of something else.*
> *But God gives it a body as he has determined,*
> *and to each kind of seed he gives its own body*
>
> 1 CORINTHIANS 15:35–38

In Heaven you will still look like you, only much, much healthier and whole. Your new body will be what it *should* have been, had Adam and Eve never sinned, only better. It will be what *could* have been if you lived on a perfect diet, breathed only pure air, exercised properly, rested well, and never had a mismanaged emotion, yet even finer. Your new body will be an improved version of all it *can* be without scars, blemishes, fat, cancers, or broken bones. It will reflect no genetic defects. Every single person in Heaven will look breathtaking and incredibly better than the most healthy and attractive person to ever walk the earth.

2. Human

When we get our new bodies, they will be improved versions of *human* bodies. In speaking of our resurrection bodies, Paul wrote,

> *All flesh is not the same: Men have one kind*
> *of flesh, animals have another, birds another and*
> *fish another.*
>
> 1 CORINTHIANS 15:39

What He is saying is that in Heaven humans will have human bodies; animals will have animal bodies; and birds will have bird bodies. When I was a little boy, I loved to watch birds fly. In fact I still do. I hoped that in Heaven I might be a bird. I won't. I won't be a panther, lion, shark, or angel, either. I will be a man with a man's body, only a much improved version of the one I have now.

3. Imperishable

In terms of age, I am north of forty. The last few years my hair has been rapidly fleeing the top of my head. The hair that still remains has become silver. Several years ago, my bottom teeth moved out of line, throwing off my bite so badly I had to wear braces (just like my youngest son—talk about a humbling experience). For the first time in my life, I have to watch my calories. I now need bifocals to read. The hair on my back, in my nose, and on my eyebrows has been growing like it is fertilized. And if that is not enough, my joints ache on rainy days. In other words, as my sons love to tell me, "Dad, you are really getting old!"

Human bodies that have not experienced the resurrection are destined to wear out, break down, and fall apart. That's bad news and a frustrating reality. But the good news is our resurrection bodies are imperishable (1 Corinthians 15:42). They won't spoil, rot, or decay. No sags or bags. No bunions, bifocals, baldness, or big bellies. Hallelujah!

4. Glorious

No one has ever accused my body of being glorious. But not only will our resurrected bodies be healthier and perpetually young, they will be downright glorious. That's right. In Heaven you will be able to look in the mirror and say, "My, my. You look glorious!" In speaking of these bodies Paul said, "It is sown in dishonor, it is raised in glory" (1 Corinthians 15:43). In Heaven Jesus won't be the only one with a royal radiance. You and I will also have a golden glow.

> *"Then the righteous will shine like the sun in the kingdom of their Father. He who has ears, let him hear."*
>
> MATTHEW 13:43

> *"Those who are wise will shine like the brightness of the heavens, and those who lead many to righteousness, like the stars for ever and ever."*
>
> DANIEL 12:3

On the Mount of Transfiguration, Peter and John got a sample of what people in Heaven will look like when they saw Jesus. The Bible says, "As he was praying, the appearance of his face changed, and his clothes became as bright as a flash of lightning" (Luke 9:29). As Moses and Elijah spoke with Him, they "appeared in glorious splendor" (Luke 9:31).

5. Powerful

In discussing the nature of a resurrection body, Paul wrote, "It is sown in weakness, it is raised in power" (1 Corinthians 15:43). One aspect of my new body I anticipate most is having new abilities.

The Bible repeatedly tells us that when Jesus appears for our resurrection, "We shall be like him, for we shall see him as he is" (1 John 3:2; see also 1 Corinthians 15:44–49). Therefore, our new bodies will be like the body the disciples saw after Jesus rose from the dead. It could appear suddenly, apparently walking through a locked door (John 20:19). It could disappear from sight (Luke 24:31). It was able to defy gravity and rise up into the clouds (Acts 1:9). Amazing!

Another of my recurring dreams is that I am flying. I never

get very high in my dreams, only about as high as the tops of the trees. I can't fly very far, but I am still flying. One day in Heaven, I may really be able to fly. My dream might come true. Wow!

6. Changed

> *Listen, I tell you a mystery: We will not all sleep, but we will all be changed—in a flash, in the twinkling of an eye, at the last trumpet. For the trumpet will sound, the dead will be raised imperishable, and we will be changed.*
>
> 1 CORINTHIANS 15:51–52

Paul was very clear. At the return of Jesus, the bodies of deceased believers will be instantly transformed. This instantaneous alteration will change us into people with wonderful resurrection bodies perfectly suited for fully accessing God and experiencing the wonders of Heaven, His home, in every dimension.

7. Immortal

As a pastor, I have learned to help grieving family members focus on eternity. We talk of the funeral service being the graduation of the deceased from Earth to Heaven. Yet, while the funeral of a saint is sweet, it is also bitter. It is so hard to say good-bye to someone we have loved.

In Heaven there will be no good-byes. There will be no morgues, funeral parlors, or cemeteries. Our amazing new bodies will never, ever die. Death will be forever left behind. The victory over death that Jesus set in process by His resurrection will be consummated at ours.

> *For the perishable must clothe itself with the imperishable, and the mortal with immortality. When the perishable has been clothed with the imperishable, and the mortal with immortality, then the saying that is written will come true: "Death has been swallowed up in victory."*
>
> *"Where, O death, is your victory? Where, O death, is your sting?" The sting of death is sin, and the power of sin is the law. But thanks be to God! He gives us the victory through our Lord Jesus Christ.*

1 CORINTHIANS 15:53–57

So What?

We can look forward to heavenly bodies similar to the ones we have now, but oh, so much better. They will not age or die. They will be radiant in perfect health and with special abilities. So how should knowing this impact our lives today? Paul answered that question for us when he concluded his lengthy discussion of the nature of our resurrection bodies with these words.

> *Therefore, my dear brothers, stand firm. Let nothing move you. Always give yourselves fully to the work of the Lord, because you know that your labor in the Lord is not in vain.*

1 CORINTHIANS 15:58

NOTES

1. Tony Campolo, "The Kingdom Is a Party," program #3315. January 14, 1990, http://www.csec.org/csec/sermon/campolo 3315.htm.

12

The Royal Wedding

On July 29, 1981, the most elegant, most talked about, most watched wedding in the history of planet Earth occurred. The fairy-tale romance of Lady Diana Spencer and Prince Charles raised worldwide interest in Britain's royal family. The heir to Britain's ancient throne and his beautiful princess-to-be obliged their admirers by holding a glittering storybook wedding with all the royal trappings imaginable. No one was disappointed.

Crowds of six hundred thousand people filled the streets of London, eager to catch even a glimpse of Prince Charles and Lady Diana on their wedding day. The couple were married at St. Paul's Cathedral before an invited congregation of thirty-five hundred and an estimated global television audience of 750 million—making it the most popular program ever broadcast. The entire nation of England enjoyed a national holiday to mark the occasion. Most people felt this was the wedding to beat all weddings, and would never be surpassed in its size, scope, and splendor.

They were wrong.

The Greatest Wedding of Them All

One day, in the not-so-distant future, Heaven will host a royal wedding that will cause the royal wedding of 1981 to be quickly forgotten. The wedding in Heaven will involve grander participants, a superior officiator, a much larger audience, and the best feast of all time. It will be called the marriage supper of the Lamb, and it is described in the book of Revelation.

> *I heard what sounded like a great multitude,*
> *like the roar of rushing waters and like loud peals*
> *of thunder, shouting: "Hallelujah! For our Lord*
> *God Almighty reigns. Let us rejoice and be glad*
> *and give him glory! For the wedding of the Lamb*
> *has come, and his bride has made herself ready.*
> *Fine linen, bright and clean, was given her to*
> *wear." (Fine linen stands for the righteous acts of*
> *the saints.) Then the angel said to me, "Write:*
> *'Blessed are those who are invited to the wedding*
> *supper of the Lamb!' " And he added, "These are*
> *the true words of God."*
>
> REVELATION 19:6–9

Heaven will host the greatest wedding of them all.

One day the streets of Heaven will resound with the joyous bells of the marriage supper of the Lamb. Using Revelation chapter 19 as the foundation, we can glean many insights into Heaven, the home of the greatest royal wedding of them all.

The Royal Bridegroom Is Jesus

This event is called the wedding *of the Lamb*. The Lamb is the Bridegroom. So who's the Lamb? Fortunately, we need not speculate. John the Baptizer told us that the Lamb is Jesus.

> *The next day John saw Jesus coming toward*
> *him, and said, "Behold! The Lamb of God who*
> *takes away the sin of the world!"*
>
> JOHN 1:29 NKJV

John wanted to clearly explain to the Jews that he was not the Messiah. He was the *forerunner* of the Messiah, the path preparer for the Messiah. John said that he was the friend of the Bridegroom, but Jesus was the Bridegroom.

> *John answered and said, "A man can receive nothing unless it has been given to him from heaven. You yourselves bear me witness, that I said, 'I am not the Christ,' but, 'I have been sent before Him.' He who has the bride is the bridegroom; but the friend of the bridegroom, who stands and hears him, rejoices greatly because of the bridegroom's voice. Therefore this joy of mine is fulfilled. He must increase, but I must decrease."*
>
> JOHN 3:27–30 NKJV

John was not the only one who knew Jesus was the Royal Bridegroom. Jesus Himself referred to Himself as the Bridegroom.

> *Then they said to Him, "Why do the disciples of John fast often and make prayers, and likewise those of the Pharisees, but Yours eat and drink?" And He said to them, "Can you make the friends of the bridegroom fast while the bridegroom is with them? But the days will come when the bridegroom will be taken away from them; then they will fast in those days."*
>
> LUKE 5:33–35 NKJV

Many thought Prince Charles made an extremely regal and

handsome groom in the full dress uniform of a British naval commander. However, the majesty of every human prince in history will pale in the splendor and glory of Prince Jesus arrayed for His wedding day.

The Bride Is the Church

In understanding the Bible, it is vital to know that when the Bible speaks of the church, it is always speaking of a designation of people, and it is never referring to a building. In fact, there were no church buildings for one hundred or more years after the birth of the church. The church has many local assemblies (I used to pastor the New Life *Church* of Gahanna, Ohio) but *the* church is one united entity made up of redeemed people of every tribe, tongue, and nation.

Just as a bride pledges supreme love and unparalleled loyalty to her husband forever, members of the church, the Bride of Christ, are those who have pledged priority love and utmost devotion to Jesus forever. It is our natural response to the sacrificial love He has already shown us. Paul wrote, "Husbands, love your wives [your brides], just as Christ also loved the church [his bride] and gave Himself for her" (Ephesians 5:25 NKJV). He also wrote, "I have betrothed you to one husband that I may present you as a chaste virgin to Christ" (2 Corinthians 11:2 NKJV).

Lady Diana made a beautiful bride. People gasped at the way her elaborate and costly dress adorned her beautiful figure. In a similar yet vastly superior way, the Bride of Jesus will be a glorious virgin, simply, yet majestically, dressed in the pure white linen of those whose sins have been washed by the blood of Jesus Christ and who show their gratitude by living righteous lives.

> *"Fine linen, bright and clean, was given her*
> *to wear." (Fine linen stands for the righteous acts*
> *of the saints.)*
>
> REVELATION 19:8

No one is exactly sure how the huge number of believers from the church era can "wed" Jesus Christ. We can assume there will be an unprecedented level of uninhibited, undisguised, unadorned unity of souls between Bride and Groom. We will enjoy complete exposure and joyous knowledge without a hint of promiscuity. We will drink deeply of pure intimacy that will not only draw us deeply to Christ, but also to each other as well.

The Guest List Will Be Impressive in Size

Lady Di and Prince Charles had thirty-five hundred invited guests. The marriage of the Lamb will have a much, much larger number in attendance. John said that he "heard what sounded like a great multitude, like the roar of rushing waters and like loud peals of thunder, shouting: 'Hallelujah!' . . .For the wedding of the Lamb has come" (Revelation 19:6–7). The guest list will include all the angels. Scripture tells us they number more than humans can count. The believers from the Old Testament era will also be glad guests at the wonderful wedding party.

God the Father Will Be the Gracious Host

Although not stated in Revelation 19, other scriptures tell us that in a unique and wonderful way, at the marriage supper of the Lamb, God the Father will serve as both the Father of the Bride and the Father of the Groom (He is *our* Father—Matthew 6:9). Because God is easily the wealthiest being in the universe, absolutely no expense will be spared. Everyone who wants to attend is welcome. There will be enough sumptuous food to last a thousand years!

Luke recorded a story Jesus told which serves as a portrait of how eager the Father is to have multitudes attend His Son's wedding. God wants everyone to be there.

> *"Then He said to him, 'A certain man gave
> a great supper and invited many, and sent his
> servant at supper time to say to those who were
> invited, "Come, for all things are now ready."
> But they all with one accord began to make
> excuses. . . . So that servant came and reported
> these things to his master. Then the master of the
> house, being angry, said to his servant, 'Go out
> quickly into the streets and lanes of the city, and
> bring in here the poor and the maimed and the
> lame and the blind.'. . .' Go out into the high-
> ways and hedges, and compel them to come in,
> that my house may be filled.' "*
>
> LUKE 14:16–18, 21, 23 NKJV

Ancient Hebrew Wedding Customs

History tells of three common elements of a Jewish wedding during the time of Christ. A look at these three elements gives us insight into the incredible celebration that will occur in Heaven.

1. The Betrothal Stage

According to the custom, during this stage in the relationship between a bride and groom, three things occur: First, the parents select a bride for the son. Second, a contract is signed. Third, the bride's father is paid a dowry. As you may recall, this was the stage Joseph and Mary were in when he found out she was pregnant. It required a divorce to break a betrothal. Fortunately, the angel told him the baby she was carrying was one miraculously conceived by God, so Joseph didn't divorce her. The rest is history.

On a spiritual level, God the Father selected a bride for His Son before the annals of time (Ephesians 1:3–4). Jesus and the

Father created a contract of commitment called the new covenant (Luke 22:20; 1 Corinthians 11:25; Hebrews 9:15). The Father gave His Son, and Jesus gave His life to pay the price for His bride (1 Corinthians 6:19–20; Ephesians 5:25). The betrothal has been fulfilled.

2. The Presentation Stage

In an ancient Hebrew wedding, the bride was fetched to the house of the groom's father for a private ceremony. One day soon, Jesus will come to get His Bride to join Him in His Father's house. Spiritually, this event has been called the Rapture of the church. Many consider it to be the next event on the prophetic calendar.

> *"In My Father's house are many mansions;*
> *if it were not so, I would have told you. I go to*
> *prepare a place for you. And if I go and prepare*
> *a place for you, I will come again and receive*
> *you to Myself; that where I am, there you may be*
> *also."*
>
> JOHN 14:2–3 NKJV

> *For the Lord Himself will descend from heaven*
> *with a shout, with the voice of an archangel, and*
> *with the trumpet of God. And the dead in Christ*
> *will rise first. Then we who are alive and remain*
> *shall be caught up together with them in the clouds*
> *to meet the Lord in the air. And thus we shall*
> *always be with the Lord.*
>
> 1 THESSALONIANS 4:16–17 NKJV

3. The Celebration Stage

In an ancient Hebrew wedding, a public party was held to celebrate the wedding. All of the friends and family were invited. These parties were huge celebrations. It was said that in those days, the party presented by a poor man would last all day; the wedding supper of the son of an average man would last close to a week; and the celebration given by a rich man would last up to a month. But the party provided by a king for his son could last for one year!

Well, friends, as they say, "you ain't seen nothin' yet." The Bible tells us that the party thrown in Heaven by God the Father for His Son, Jesus Christ, the King of kings and Lord of lords, will not be a one-day affair. It won't last a mere week or month; it will not last a year. No, there is a strong possibility that the marriage of the Lamb, given by God the Father for His son, King Jesus, and His daughter, the Bride of Christ, will last one thousand years (Revelation 20:1–6)!

So What?

What good does knowing this do us now? It certainly gives us something marvelous to look forward to. It gives us hope. Sometimes Christians look at people in the world who are godless and who seem to party their lives away, and we feel a twinge of envy. We ponder, "Why do the ungodly get to have all the fun?"

Friend, if you miss a few decades, worth of parties down here, don't worry. God is going to throw us a thousand-year party up there!

13

THE ROYAL KINGDOM

Do you ever get tired of living on a rebel planet? I do.

Let me explain.

When Adam and Eve introduced sin and rebellion to Earth way back in the Garden of Eden, they unwittingly handed Satan the title deed to the planet. Since then, Satan, the usurper prince, has lived as god of this world and prince of the power of the air. Under his wicked reign, sickness, sorrow, sadness, disease, destruction, debauchery, and death have polluted the planet and enslaved its citizens. His reign of terror has been building in these last days, and it will reach a horrible zenith during the seven years of tribulation. But fear not: Lucifer, the pretender prince, is on a short lease. His downfall is certain and soon.

For thousands of years, King Jesus has lived as a monarch in exile (John 18:36–37). He briefly visited His planet to shed His royal blood to free an army of loyal subjects (Revelation 5:9). One day very soon, in the climactic battle of Armageddon, He will return to Earth to claim His throne and restore His kingdom (Revelation 19:11–21; Psalm 2; Zechariah 14:3–5). At this time Heaven will, in a sense, be relocated to Earth as a glorious kingdom.

Heaven will be a glorious kingdom ruled by King Jesus.

King of Kings and Lord of Lords

When Jesus returns to Earth to establish His kingdom, it will not be a quiet, political, on-paper transfer of power. No way! Satan will not let go easily and will fight Jesus with every weapon at his disposal, including all the armies of Earth. Jesus left Earth as a Lamb slain for our sins, but He will return as the Lion of the tribe of Judah, dressed in full battle array, to put down the enemy insurrection.

> *I saw heaven standing open and there before me was a white horse, whose rider is called Faithful and True. With justice he judges and makes war. His eyes are like blazing fire, and on his head are many crowns. He has a name written on him that no one knows but he himself. He is dressed in a robe dipped in blood, and his name is the Word of God. The armies of heaven were following him, riding on white horses and dressed in fine linen, white and clean. Out of his mouth comes a sharp sword with which to strike down the nations. He will rule them with an iron scepter. He treads the winepress of the fury of the wrath of God Almighty. On his robe and on his thigh he has this name written:* KING OF KINGS AND LORD OF LORDS.

> REVELATION 19:11–16

After Satan and his cohorts-in-crime are defeated, they will be punished for all of the pain they wreaked on the innocent. The devil will be sentenced to one thousand years of hard time. During that millennium, King Jesus will reign on Earth.

> *And I saw an angel coming down out of
> heaven, having the key to the Abyss and holding
> in his hand a great chain. He seized the dragon,
> that ancient serpent, who is the devil, or Satan,
> and bound him for a thousand years. He threw
> him into the Abyss, and locked and sealed it over
> him, to keep him from deceiving the nations any-
> more until the thousand years were ended.*

> REVELATION 20:1–3

A Kingdom of Prosperity and Peace

I have never been overly impressed with earthly governments. As long as sinful humans are in control, ignorance and incompetence can and will occur. Power, corruption, and greed have decayed and destroyed countless earthly kingdoms. As a result, rank and file citizens suffer. But, one day King Jesus will establish an excellent, everlasting kingdom on earth (2 Samuel 7:16; Micah 4:7–8).

> *The LORD will be king over the whole earth.
> On that day there will be one LORD, and his
> name the only name.*

> ZECHARIAH 14:9

Israel will be renewed as the center of world power. Jerusalem will serve as the home base of His glorious kingdom.

> *For the LORD Almighty will reign on Mount
> Zion and in Jerusalem, and before its elders,
> gloriously.*

> ISAIAH 24:23

The kingdom of Jesus will be unlike any other kingdom. It will have a perfect, supremely sinless, radically righteous, just, wise, kind, benevolent leader—Jesus Christ the Lord. Those ruling under Him will be perfected saints who left their sinful natures behind when they stepped into eternity.

It will be wonderful to be a citizen of the kingdom ruled by Jesus. Imagine how nice it will be to live in a beautiful country that is amazingly absent of illogical, unreasonable, needless layers of red tape. What a joy it will be to live in a place devoid of divisive, partisan politics and the bribery of special interest groups. Imagine a government completely lacking power-hungry politicians and out-of-touch, uncaring bureaucrats.

Jesus' kingdom will be marked by unprecedented peace and prosperity in every area of life. Previously inconceivable animal, civil, political, military, and social tranquility will rule the day. It will be heavenly.

> *The wolf will live with the lamb, the leopard will lie down with the goat, the calf and the lion and the yearling together; and a little child will lead them. The cow will feed with the bear, their young will lie down together, and the lion will eat straw like the ox. The infant will play near the hole of the cobra, and the young child put his hand into the viper's nest. They will neither harm nor destroy on all my holy mountain, for the earth will be full of the knowledge of the LORD as the waters cover the sea. In that day the Root of Jesse will stand as a banner for the peoples; the nations will rally to him, and his place of rest will be glorious.*
>
> ISAIAH 11:6–10

> *He will judge between many peoples and will*
> *settle disputes for strong nations far and wide.*
> *They will beat their swords into plowshares and*
> *their spears into pruning hooks. Nation will not*
> *take up sword against nation, nor will they train*
> *for war anymore. Every man will sit under his*
> *own vine and under his own fig tree, and no one*
> *will make them afraid, for the LORD Almighty*
> *has spoken.*
>
> MICAH 4:3–4

During this season, Israelis will return to their Messiah and experience unprecedented prosperity in their land.

> *Sing, O Daughter of Zion; shout aloud, O*
> *Israel! Be glad and rejoice with all your heart, O*
> *Daughter of Jerusalem! The LORD has taken away*
> *your punishment, he has turned back your enemy.*
> *The LORD, the King of Israel, is with you; never*
> *again will you fear any harm. . . . At that time I*
> *will deal with all who oppressed you; I will rescue*
> *the lame and gather those who have been scattered.*
> *I will give them praise and honor in every land*
> *where they were put to shame.*
>
> ZEPHANIAH 3:14–15, 19

We Will Reign with Him

Jesus will receive wonderful worship in Heaven because He is genuinely worth it. He not only purchased us out of the slave market of sin by His blood, but He also made it possible for us one day to rule with Him on the earth.

> *And they sang a new song: "You are worthy*
> *to take the scroll and to open its seals, because you*
> *were slain, and with your blood you purchased*
> *men for God from every tribe and language and*
> *people and nation. You have made them to be a*
> *kingdom and priests to serve our God, and they*
> *will reign on the earth."*
>
> REVELATION 5:9–10

John heard them singing that those purchased by the blood of the Lamb would one day "reign on the earth" (Revelation 5:9). Paul reminded his readers, "If we endure, we will also reign with him" (2 Timothy 2:12). Jesus told a story indicating that those who handled their God-given responsibilities and resources wisely would one day "take charge" of cities (Luke 19:11–27).

It seems that I have been leading one group of people or another all of my adult life. There are several aspects or situations of leadership that make it extremely draining and discouraging. One, for example, is trying to lead while serving under an incompetent, corrupt, or uncaring boss. This problem will be removed in the kingdom of the Lord Jesus, as He will be the perfect superior, completely capable, incredibly incorruptible, and having the greatest heart for humanity in the universe.

Another frustrating aspect of governance is seldom having enough resources to do the job right. Again, this will not be a difficulty in Heaven, as our kingdom will have every resource on the renewed planet at our disposal.

I also find leading imperfect people can be one of the most infuriating tasks one can undertake. Leading self-oriented people can be like herding cats—nearly impossible and often frustrating. But in the kingdom of the Son, we will have the opportunity to lead perfected, glorified people, who have left their egos and agendas behind. Their problem-causing baggage of hurts, hang-ups, and nasty habits will be long gone.

Responsibility Is Earned

During the last week of Jesus' earthly life, many people thought He was going to establish His kingdom on earth very soon (Luke 19:11). In trying to adjust their expectations, Jesus told a story related to His coming kingdom.

> *"A man of noble birth went to a distant country to have himself appointed king and then to return. So he called ten of his servants and gave them ten minas. 'Put this money to work,' he said, 'until I come back.' "*
>
> LUKE 19:12–13

A mina was worth a lot of money—about three months' worth of salary. If you make fifty thousand dollars a year, three months of salary would be $12,500. Each of these servants received *ten* times that amount to invest for their master.

> *"He was made king. . .and returned home. Then he sent for the servants to whom he had given the money, in order to find out what they had gained with it. The first one came and said, 'Sir, your mina has earned ten more.'*
> *" 'Well done, my good servant!' his master replied. 'Because you have been trustworthy in a very small matter, take charge of ten cities.'*
> *"The second came and said, 'Sir, your mina has earned five more.' His master answered, 'You take charge of five cities.' "*
>
> LUKE 19:15–19

Jesus makes it clear that the key to future kingdom responsibility is wise use of what He has already given us here on Earth. If we maximize and use our time, treasures, and talents for Him and His kingdom, then we will have a better role in the royal kingdom. But if we don't, we won't.

> *"Then another servant came and said, 'Sir, here is your mina; I have kept it laid away in a piece of cloth. I was afraid of you, because you are a hard man. You take out what you did not put in and reap what you did not sow.'*
>
> *"His master replied, 'I will judge you by your own words, you wicked servant! You knew, did you, that I am a hard man, taking out what I did not put in, and reaping what I did not sow? Why then didn't you put my money on deposit, so that when I came back, I could have collected it with interest?'*
>
> *Then he said to those standing by, 'Take his mina away from him and give it to the one who has ten minas.'*
>
> *"'Sir,' they said, 'he already has ten!'*
>
> *"He replied, 'I tell you that to everyone who has, more will be given, but as for the one who has nothing, even what he has will be taken away.'"*
>
> LUKE 19:20–26

So What?

Having a lousy job is. . .well. . .lousy. It is a daily frustration. I know because I have had a few, and most likely so have you. While there will be no miserable jobs in the royal kingdom, some positions will be better than others. If I want to guarantee myself the best possible role in the royal kingdom, I must try to live my life wisely and well, using everything God has put at my disposal responsibly for Him.

14

THE ROYAL CITY

Cities display humanity at its very best and its absolute worst. Cities have the greatest highways but also the nastiest traffic. In a city, you can be treated by the finest medical specialists yet sit for hours in the waiting rooms of the most impersonal physicians. Cities offer museums filled with breathtaking, amazing pieces of art and also galleries cluttered with outrageously offensive objects.

Only in cities can you choose between dozens of outstanding restaurants as you drive by projects where children go to bed hungry. Only in cities can you walk by homeless men begging on the street as you enter a five-star hotel.

Per capita, cities employ the most police to protect the citizens, but that is because they have the most criminals. You will find the irony of stately old church buildings with working prostitutes outside on the sidewalk, soliciting clients on Friday nights.

Cities have mass transit and mass hysteria, remarkable affluence and marked apathy. Only in cities can you see hundreds of thousands of people, but often no one to lend a hand. The loneliest people on Earth often live in the most populated cities. In cities, we look up and gasp as we witness the fruit of man scaling the heights of his architectural and constructive achievement, only to trip over a broken-down bum stumbling around drunk or sleeping in the stench of his own vomit.

Can the potential good of the city ever be harnessed for God? Certainly, but there is only who can pull it off: His name is Jesus. Following the millennial kingdom, He will reveal the grandest, greatest, most glorious city that anyone has ever seen or imagined. It is called New Jerusalem and it will be the capital of New Heaven.

One day Heaven will have a glorious capital city.

The Holy City

The apostle John had the incomparable privilege of seeing into the future of both Earth and Heaven. Those two futures will one day gloriously collide in a realm known as New Heaven, New Earth, and New Jerusalem.

> *Then I saw a new heaven and a new earth,*
> *for the first heaven and the first earth had passed*
> *away, and there was no longer any sea. I saw the*
> *Holy City, the new Jerusalem, coming down out*
> *of heaven from God.*
>
> REVELATION 21:1–2

> *"He who overcomes will inherit all this, and*
> *I will be his God and he will be my son. But the*
> *cowardly, the unbelieving, the vile, the murderers,*
> *the sexually immoral, those who practice magic*
> *arts, the idolaters and all liars—their place will*
> *be in the fiery lake of burning sulfur. This is the*
> *second death."*
>
> REVELATION 21:7–8

> *Nothing impure will ever enter it, nor will*
> *anyone who does what is shameful or deceitful, but*
> *only those whose names are written in the Lamb's*
> *book of life.*
>
> REVELATION 21:27

The word *holy* in the Greek language means "separate from sin." New Jerusalem will be the first truly *holy* city to ever exist on Earth. It will be a place without sin. As such, it will have every single good thing about large cities, but absolutely none of the bad. There will be culture without crime and people without pollution. There will be decency with dignity, purity with power, and greatness with goodness. Happiness and harmony will flood each heart, fill the air, and flow down every street.

New Jerusalem will have no active muggers, burglars, thieves, con artists, pornographers, pimps, drug dealers, rapists, arsonists, or murderers. It will, of course, have former felons who have been forgiven by Jesus. New Jerusalem will be gloriously void of jails, prisons, and courtrooms. Lawyers, district attorneys, judges, bailiffs, police officers, and detectives will either have different roles to play or will find entirely different lines of work.

Imagine living in a city where you won't have to lock your doors when you go out or deadbolt them when you stay in. Imagine being able to walk down any street, any time, without fear of urban predators. Imagine great quantities of good food, good fun, and good times enjoyed in the company of very good people. New Jerusalem will be all of that and so much more.

The Perpetually New City

Many, if not all, of the major metropolitan cities in America have crumbling sections of their inner city. Once-regal buildings slowly rot and deteriorate. Plumbing is bad and often ineffective. Wiring is outdated and unsafe. Roaches and rats thrive in the revolting filth and repulsive stench that crowd the alleys and flood the basements.

But New Jerusalem will have none of these depressing and dangerous divisions of downtown. God will make "everything new!" (Revelation 21:5). Every wire and window, fiber and floor, of every single building and block, will be entirely fresh, clean, bright, and brand spanking new! And I believe Jesus has the creative ability and knack of making it perpetually new, throughout eternity. Imagine being in a place that is always familiar, yet fresh—that will be New Jerusalem.

The Beautiful New City

Twenty years ago, if you walked down the streets of Moscow, the capital of the former Soviet Union, you would have discovered that decades of godless tyranny had literally drained color out of the skyline. Apart from the brightly colored spheres of the domes of the Kremlin, every building sagged in depressing shades of gray and brown. Hunched-over citizens dragged down the dreary streets draped in dull, tired clothes. Drab clouds hung in the air, straining out the life and brightness of the sun. Happiness was hard to find, as though joy had been outlawed.

Yet, by the mid-nineties, the positive impact of perestroika was beginning to be visible. Here and there a radiant red scarf or an effervescent blue tie would sprinkle the otherwise bland backdrop. Girls' dresses of vivacious greens and vibrant yellows began to break the otherwise monotonous grey of the city. It is amazing what a little freedom did for the face of that city. Imagine what true freedom will do to the city of God.

New Jerusalem was described by John as undoubtedly the most stunning city anyone has ever seen. Rising majestically on a lofty mountain, it will radiate in the golden glow of the glory of God. Color and light will commingle to create an awesome, inspiring, delightful feast for the eyes. Every color of the rainbow will be stretched, massaged, and empowered to levels man has never witnessed. Using a palette of pure gold, clear crystal, and precious stones, Jesus will paint His city into a massive masterpiece.

> *I saw the Holy City, the new Jerusalem, coming down out of heaven from God, prepared as a bride beautifully dressed for her husband.*
>
> REVELATION 21:2

> *One of the seven angels who had the seven bowls full of the seven last plagues came and said to me, "Come, I will show you the bride, the wife of the Lamb." And he carried me away in the Spirit to a mountain great and high, and showed me the Holy City, Jerusalem, coming down out of heaven from God. It shone with the glory of God, and its brilliance was like that of a very precious jewel, like a jasper, clear as crystal.*
>
> REVELATION 21:9–11

> *The wall was made of jasper, and the city of pure gold, as pure as glass. The foundations of the city walls were decorated with every kind of precious stone. The first foundation was jasper, the second sapphire, the third chalcedony, the fourth emerald, the fifth sardonyx, the sixth carnelian, the seventh chrysolite, the eighth beryl, the ninth topaz, the tenth chrysoprase, the eleventh jacinth, and the twelfth amethyst. The twelve gates were twelve pearls, each gate made of a single pearl. The great street of the city was of pure gold, like transparent glass.*
>
> REVELATION 21:18–21

The City of Life

The downtowns of many large cities are dying. Abandoned stores, empty restaurants, and collapsing buildings dot the landscape. Jobs are scarce and business is disappearing. But New Jerusalem will be full of life and prosperity.

Most cities were born because of their prime location along either seaboards or water routes. Even today, the geography of many cities is defined by a river. Even though it stands on a mountain, New Jerusalem will pulsate with the crystal clear river of life. The banks of the river will be graced by the tree of life. This miraculous tree yields perpetual wonder fruit that will give all who eat it continual youth and life. Its leaves will somehow have the capacity to bring health and healing.

> *Then the angel showed me the river of the water of life, as clear as crystal, flowing from the throne of God and of the Lamb down the middle of the great street of the city. On each side of the river stood the tree of life, bearing twelve crops of fruit, yielding its fruit every month. And the leaves of the tree are for the healing of the nations. No longer will there be any curse.*
>
> REVELATION 22:1–3

The City of Light

> *The city does not need the sun or the moon to shine on it, for the glory of God gives it light, and the Lamb is its lamp. The nations will walk by its light, and the kings of the earth will bring their splendor into it. On no day will its gates ever be shut, for there will be no night there. The glory and honor of the nations will be brought into it.*
>
> REVELATION 21:23–26

> *There will be no more night. They will not*
> *need the light of a lamp or the light of the sun,*
> *for the Lord God will give them light.*
>
> REVELATION 22:5

Picture a place without darkness. Imagine a city that needs no streetlights, lamps, house lights, headlights, flashlights, night lights, or chandeliers. Envision a municipality that is wonderfully warmed and lit without the aid of the sun. New Jerusalem will be such a place. Because God makes His residence there and manifests His presence in an unhindered, uninhibited, unlimited way, His very being will give Heaven an ongoing, glorious, golden glow. It will be a city lit by the light of the Lamb. There will be nothing to fear and nothing to hide.

The Gigantic City

John was not only struck by the beauty of the glorious city of God. He also was told to carefully note its immense and unique dimensions.

> *The angel who talked with me had a mea-*
> *suring rod of gold to measure the city, its gates*
> *and its walls. The city was laid out like a square,*
> *as long as it was wide. He measured the city*
> *with the rod and found it to be 12,000 stadia*
> *in length, and as wide and high as it is long. He*
> *measured its wall and it was 144 cubits thick, by*
> *man's measurement, which the angel was using.*
>
> REVELATION 21:15–17

John measured a city that was 12,000 stadia (1,400 miles) long and wide, making New Jerusalem 1.96 million square miles! Such an immense city would surpass any city man has ever known. It will be larger than most countries. New Jerusalem will be nearly *nine thousand* times the size of Chicago. It will be over *six thousand* times the size of New York City. It will be nearly *four hundred* times the size of the state of Texas, nearly ten times the size of France, and over half the size of China. That is one huge city. But that's not all John saw.

The city John saw was also 1,400 *miles* high! The tallest building in America is the Sears Tower in downtown Chicago. It is 1,450 *feet* tall, 110 stories high. There are 5,280 feet in a mile, making New Jerusalem 7.39 million feet high and over 5,000 times taller than the Sears tower! It could theoretically house more than half a million stories, nearly two million square miles each.

Some say that New Jerusalem will be a colossal cube, others a giant pyramid. Either way, it will certainly be big enough to spaciously house and feed a mammoth population. None of the numbers discussed even addresses the new Heaven and the new Earth. There is definitely plenty of room for all who want to be in Heaven to live comfortably and well.

So What?

New Jerusalem will be a gorgeous, gigantic, holy city full of life and light. It will have everything good any city in history has ever had, plus much more, while at the same time having none of the bad. It will be *the* place to spend eternity. You will not want to miss it.

15

GOD'S HOUSE

There is little we need other than God Himself.

A. W. TOZER[1]

We Need God

Every person who lives on this planet now, lived on this planet in the past, or will live on this planet in the future has one common characteristic. The unanimous, universal denominator linking us all is a gaping, God-shaped void in our hearts. When He made us, He made us to have a holy hunger for Him.

This sacred space has been violated and twisted by the curse of sin. As a result, instead of seeking to fill our yawning empti-ness with God, we easily settle for substitutes. Some of these surrogate gods are decidedly negative and dangerously addic-tive. Everyone knows dependency on drugs, alcohol, gambling, pornography, or illicit sex can never satisfy. Other alternatives are neutral entities. Money, work, career, achievement, hobbies, food, and material things are only evil when we expect them to take the place of God. Then they fall pathetically short.

Most of us suffer from the continual temptation to put very good entities in our God void. We all attest to the intrinsic value of family, friends, church, and ministry. Yet when we try to place even these good entities into the God-shaped space in our hearts, inevitable emptiness comes. Why? Nothing or no one can replace God. Only God can fill the holy hole in our hearts. Everything else is, at best, a square peg in a round hole or, better yet, a tiny pebble in an infinite chasm.

We need God. One 100 percent pure God is our deepest need and greatest fulfillment. Clearly, nothing else can compare with infinite perfection. The very best of all things is *God.* With God you have all things. Without God you have nothing.[2]

The great appeal of Heaven is more than the incredible beauty, astounding wealth, or fantastic fun we will experience there. It is the infinite God. The bottom line is that Heaven is about *God.* Maybe you want to go to Heaven because you were looking for something that seems to be missing. Let me tell you, that something is a *Someone*—God! What you really crave is found by experiencing more of Him—more often, more deeply, more intimately, and more powerfully—than you imagined possible. We experience tiny tastes of Him on Earth, but heaping spoonfuls in Heaven. That is why it is Heaven.

In this book, we learn twenty-one of the best truths about Heaven. But absolutely, undeniably, and unquestionably the most significant truth anyone can grasp about Heaven is this: God will be there. Heaven is God's home, and we will see Him face to face.

Heaven is God's home.

Jesus encouraged His disciples by telling them about His Father's house.

> *"In my Father's house are many rooms; if it were not so, I would have told you. I am going there to prepare a place for you."*
>
> JOHN 14:2

When the apostle John saw into Heaven, the central feature was not the tree of life or the crystal sea. It was God.

> *I saw the Holy City, the new Jerusalem, coming down out of heaven from God. . . . And I heard a loud voice from the throne saying, "Now the dwelling of God is with men, and he will live with them. They will be his people, and God himself will be with them and be their God."*
>
> REVELATION 21:2–3

> *I did not see a temple in the city, because the Lord God Almighty and the Lamb are its temple.*
>
> REVELATION 21:22

> *The throne of God and of the Lamb will be in the city.*
>
> REVELATION 22:3

Heaven Is God's Home

The beat drumming throughout the Bible is that Heaven is the dwelling place of God. Moses prayed, "Look down from *heaven, your holy dwelling place*, and bless your people Israel" (Deuteronomy 26:15, emphasis added). Jesus told us to pray to "Our Father *in heaven*" (Matthew 6:9, emphasis added). John saw the Father sitting on His throne (Revelation 4:2–9). Jesus claimed that as the Son of God, He "came down from heaven" (John 6:42). Forty days after His resurrection, He ascended visibly back to Heaven (Acts 1:9–11). He will one day return to Earth from Heaven (Revelation 19:11–16). Heaven is the dwelling place of God.

One of the very best aspects of having a home is being in a place where you can be yourself. You can relax. You do not have to hold back. You can fully express yourself.

Heaven will be astoundingly amazing because, as His home, it is the only place in the universe where God is free to fully express Himself. In Heaven God holds nothing in reserve. Nothing is limited by the presence of sin. God can be Himself. All of His goodness, all of His grandeur, all of His greatness, all of His generosity, and all of His magnificent glory can be let out. Everything His infinite heart has held in check since the creation of the universe can be conveyed.

In their own home, people reveal their true selves. Their hobbies, humor, personalities, passions, and pursuits are unveiled. At home, in Heaven, the Lord's personality, humor, dreams, and desires will be evident.

We Will See Him Face to Face

Moses begged God for a glimpse of His glory. Knowing that a direct look at His glory would be much more than Moses could safely comprehend, God suggested a plan.

> Then Moses said, "Now show me your glory."
> And the LORD said, "I will cause all my goodness to pass in front of you, and I will proclaim my name, the LORD, in your presence. . . . But," he said, "you cannot see my face, for no one may see me and live."
> Then the LORD said, "There is a place near me where you may stand on a rock. When my glory passes by, I will put you in a cleft in the rock and cover you with my hand until I have passed by. Then I will remove my hand and you will see my back."
>
> EXODUS 33:18–23

Moses was given a privilege no one else in his day could ever hope for. He received an unprecedented look at God's back. But every single person in Heaven will get to see God face to face (Revelation 22:3–4).

For those of us who proudly line up in the company of God seekers, the mere whisper of seeing our God face to face sends shivers down our spines. For so many years, we have worshiped a God we have never seen. As His children, we have often heard the comfort of our Father's voice, but we have never been allowed to sit in His lap, look into His eyes, or touch His face. We have tried to be loyal servants, faithfully fulfilling the wishes of a Master we have yet to see. As dutiful soldiers, we have gladly laid down our lives for our King, yet our eyes have yet to see His throne. As His betrothed Bride we have received many gifts from His hands and letters of love from His pen, yet what we long for is our wedding day. Then we will dance in His arms, be consumed by His love, and gaze into His eyes.

It's the Person Who Makes the Place

What makes Heaven so amazing is not merely the stunning streets of gold, the gates of pearl, the radiant light, the crystal river of life, or the everyday association with angels. It is not merely receiving a great new body, enjoying the absence of sickness and death, experiencing the reunion with loved ones, or basking in the majestic magnificence of the Master's throne—although each is amazingly impressive. What makes Heaven heavenly is not the *place,* it is the *person.* Heaven is heavenly because the Lord lives there.

Heaven is the only place where God's presence is revealed in an unlimited fashion. In Heaven God's presence is unhindered and unrestricted. Heaven is all God, all the time. That is what makes it so heavenly.

The Bible clearly tells us that God is love (1 John 4:8, 16).

Since Heaven is the only place where God's presence is fully expressed, the very atmosphere of Heaven will be swimming in the pure, good, deep, rich, wonderful love of God. Just breathing the oxygen of God's love in the air will heal our deepest hurts and soothe our greatest fears.

God is also light (1 John 1:5). Because Heaven is the place where God dwells unhindered and unrestricted, Heaven will radiate in the brilliant, perpetual light of His glory. Sun, moon, and stars will be unnecessary there.

> *The city does not need the sun or the moon*
> *to shine on it, for the glory of God gives it light,*
> *and the Lamb is its lamp. The nations will walk*
> *by its light, and the kings of the earth will bring*
> *their splendor into it. On no day will its gates*
> *ever be shut, for there will be no night there.*
>
> REVELATION 21:23–25

> *There will be no more night. They will not*
> *need the light of a lamp or the light of the sun,*
> *for the Lord God will give them light.*
>
> REVELATION 22:5

As God is creative, excellent, loving, joyful, encouraging, faithful, true, good, and holy, so is Heaven a marvelously holy place, overflowing with all that is beautiful and truly excellent, running over with love, joy, encouragement, truth, and peace. Heaven is the sphere where the heavenly presence of God is unleashed.

So What?

The insightful twentieth-century prophet A. W. Tozer said, "The man who has God for his treasure has all through One."[3] Everyone in Heaven will be astoundingly rich because the Lord will be our treasure. Our capacity to enjoy and appreciate this privilege will be expanded and enhanced to the extent that we make God our primary passion now.

NOTES

1. A. W. Tozer, *The Pursuit of God* (Camp Hill, Pennsylvania: Christian Publications, 1982), 7
2. Dave Earley, *Living in His Presence*, (Minneapolis: Bethany House, 2005), 9
3. Tozer, 19.

16

YOUR FINAL FORWARDING ADDRESS

Heaven is better than anything we can imagine, and it will get even better. From Paradise to the Royal Kingdom, Heaven will be renovated, re-created, expanded, and improved. The last phase of Heaven described in the Bible is the new Heaven and new Earth. After the millennium will come the final purging of Earth. This will birth the re-creation and the wedding of Heaven and Earth. The capital will be New Jerusalem. We have already talked about the giant royal city, New Jerusalem. In this chapter, we want to discuss what the rest of New Heaven will be like.

As I read what the scriptures say about New Heaven and meditate on it through the lens of a sanctified imagination, several adjectives crystallize and summarize what it will be like to be in New Heaven.

Heaven will ultimately be a God-filled, pleasure-packed, fresh, thirst-quenching inheritance, available to all who truly want to be there.

God Filled

As we said in the previous chapter, New Heaven will be marvelously enhanced by the manifest presence of God. God will set up shop right in the middle of town (Revelation 21:1, 3; 22:3–4). What makes Heaven heavenly? It is God. It is having easy access, close proximity, and refreshing closeness to God. Everything else we can say, think, or feel about Heaven will pale compared to seeing His face, looking in His eyes, and hearing His voice. Imagine sitting down and talking to Jesus, opening your eyes, finding Him right there looking at you, and drinking in every word. Imagine being able to finally ask Him every question that has plagued your thoughts.

New Heaven is where God's creative, excellent, living, loving, joyful, encouraging, faithful, true, good, and holy presence flows. New Heaven will be adorned by the distinctive aura of God punctuating and permeating everything about it.

Pleasure Packed

> *"He will wipe every tear from their eyes. There will be no more death or mourning or crying or pain, for the old order of things has passed away."*

> REVELATION 21:4

Imagine never having your heart broken again. Consider what it will be like to never have to say good-bye to a loved one again. Imagine no more bitter, angry tears. Picture a life without pain. How wonderful it will be never to have to stand aside helplessly while someone else suffers.

New Heaven will be a continual celebration of the ultimate and absolute amputation of every evil or painful aspect of life that accompanied the curse of sin. The spoils of Jesus' victory over the grave will be on continual display. Death will be decisively defeated and deleted. Grief and guilt will be gloriously gone, all gone. Fear will be forbidden. Mourning will permanently turn to dancing, sorrow to joy, pain to pleasure, and misery to celebration.

Love will reign supreme. Peace will flow like water.

In New Heaven suffering must say, "So long, farewell," gloom, "Good-bye," and shame, "See you later." There will be no more anxiety, no more anguish, no more tears. Heartache, misery, sadness, and depression will be eternally ejected. In Heaven contentment will consume your emotions and satisfy your soul.

Fresh

One man was upset to find that his death was mistakenly noted in the local paper. He hastened to the editor to protest. "I'm awfully sorry," said the editor, "and it's too late to do much about it. The best thing I can do for you is to put you in tomorrow's birth column and give you a brand-new start."

New Heaven will be an everlasting morning and perpetually brand-new start.

> *He who was seated on the throne said, "I am making everything new!" Then he said, "Write this down, for these words are trustworthy and true."*
>
> REVELATION 21:5

If you live above the Mason-Dixon line, the coming of spring has mysterious power. Magically, the dormant earth awakens to new life. Grass begins to grow again, flowers poke their heads out of clean-smelling dirt, and buds boldly sprout on the trees. Birds sing before sunup like there is no tomorrow. New moms proudly push their new babies down the street in brand-new strollers.

The air is fresh, the colors ignited, the earth reborn.

Everyone is in a good mood. Everything smells fresh and clean. Everywhere there is new hope. Winter is over. Cold, cloudy skies have been conquered by clear, sunny, warm days. The aroma of honeysuckle graces the air. Ahh—I love spring.

But, amazingly, in a way that will never get old, New Heaven will be an eternal spring. The vibrant, fresh feeling that permeates the atmosphere at spring will saturate Heaven. Forgotten dreams will be reborn. Old, broken relationships will be restored. Deep passions will be rekindled. Everything will be made new.

Thirst Quenching

We all live with a cavernous craving for something we cannot quite comprehend. No matter how intensely we strive, somewhere just beyond our grasp is something we long for. This gnawing yearning, this profound passion, this deep desire drives the sensitive among us to distraction or despair. What is this vague something that we know we have tasted, but realize we never have enough of? What is this mysterious motivation and terrible thirst?

Is it love? Or maybe truth? How about peace? Maybe what we really want is true happiness? Do we yearn for rest, or affirmation, or stability, or security? Or is it intimacy, or maybe acclaim, or attention? Could our hearts be longing after adventure, excitement, or thrill? What about life, eternal life, the fountain of youth? Is that it?

The answer is yes. . .and no. What we really crave, yet so often fail to recognize and always fail to satisfy, is a hunger for Heaven. It is God and all that comes from being close to Him. It is the life, real life, the eternal life that He gives. It is only fulfilled in Heaven.

One of the very best things about Heaven is that the annoying, frustrating, inner thirst that will never be fully quenched down here and now will be fully quenched in New Heaven. Jesus promised:

*"To him who is thirsty I will give to drink
without cost from the spring of the water of life."*

REVELATION 21:6

Inheritance

According to *Forbes* magazine, the richest person on Earth is
Bill Gates, the founder of Microsoft. His net worth is fifty billion dollars—that is a five plus ten zeroes! Gates is a self-made
man who dropped out of college to start a computer company
thirty years ago. If he were to divide his wealth among his three
children, they would each be among the richest people on
Earth.[1]

Sam Walton began as a JCPenney clerk but opened his first
discount store in Rogers, Arkansas, in 1962. His little store,
Wal-Mart, has become the world's largest retailer, with more
than 5,100 stores serving 138 million customers per week.
At his death in 1992, each of his four children received over
five billion dollars. They are now worth over three times that
amount.[2]

The Bible is very clear that we are the heirs of God. In
Heaven we have an inheritance waiting for us. We will be the
heirs of God Himself, who has promised,

*"He who overcomes will inherit all this, and
I will be his God and he will be my son."*

REVELATION 21:7

*Now if we are children, then we are heirs—
heirs of God and co-heirs with Christ.*

ROMANS 8:17

> *Praise be to the God and Father of our Lord*
> *Jesus Christ! In his great mercy he has given us*
> *new birth into a living hope through the resur-*
> *rection of Jesus Christ from the dead, and into*
> *an inheritance that can never perish, spoil or*
> *fade—kept in heaven for you.*
>
> 1 PETER 1:3–4

Our inheritance could easily dwarf anything anyone on Earth has ever received. How much will we inherit in Heaven? The answer is easy. We will inherit exactly the amount that is best for us and exactly the amount we deserve. If we were generous in making eternal investments in Heaven, God will be generous in giving us our inheritance in Heaven (Matthew 6:19–21).

According to *Forbes,* Updown Court, Windlesham, England, is currently the most expensive residence on the market in the world with an asking price of $122 million. The brand-new property is totally over the top, with 103 rooms, five swimming pools, and 24-carat gold leafing on the study's mosaic floor. There's a squash court, bowling alley, tennis court, 50-seat screening room, heated marble driveway, and helipad. All eight of your limousines will fit in the underground garage. The neighbors include the Queen of England at Windsor Castle.[3]

Jesus promised us special dwellings connected to the Father's house.

> *"In My Father's house are many dwelling*
> *places; if it were not so, I would have told you;*
> *for I go to prepare a place for you."*
>
> JOHN 14:2 NASB

We don't know much more about these residences, but we can be sure that they will be exactly the best size, style, shape, and location for us. In our heavenly homes, we will enjoy being neighbors with the King—that is King Jesus, the King of kings and the Lord of lords!

Available

> *The Spirit and the bride say, "Come!" And let him who hears say, "Come!" Whoever is thirsty, let him come; and whoever wishes, let him take the free gift of the water of life.*
>
> REVELATION 22:17

Apart from God being there, one of the greatest points about Heaven is its amazing availability to all who truly want in. Granted, I realize that some people don't want 100 percent of God 100 percent of the time. Some people have no stomach for good, clean fun. Some are repulsed by the thought of endless morning, perpetual beauty, and never-ending spring. Some hate worship, mock truth, and discount or deny Jesus. The bottom line is they simply don't want to be in Heaven.

Don't worry.

God won't make them go. Heaven is only available to those who really *want* to be there. It is *free* to those who will receive the free gift of the water of life, by expressed faith in Jesus Christ the Lord.

So What?

The new Heaven will be a God-filled, pleasure-packed, new, thirst-quenching inheritance available to all who truly want to be there. The big question for us to ask ourselves is this: Do we love God enough to want to spend eternity with Him? If so, we can. You can come to Him right now in prayer. Tell Him that you want to spend eternity with Him. Tell Him you want to drink deeply of the free gift of the water of life. If you really mean it, reservations will be made for you in Heaven.

NOTES

1. Luisa Kroll and Allison Fass, ed. "The World's Billionaires" (March 9, 2006), http://www.forbes.com/billionaires.
2. "Freeze and Squeeze," http://gift-estate.com/article/Freeze.htm.
3. Sara Clemence, "The Most Expensive Homes in the World," http://www.forbes.com/2005/07/26/cx_sc_0729home_eu.html?thisSpeed=6000.

17

ANGEL ASSOCIATES

You are not alone. I would guess that this very moment invisible visitors are viewing your every movement. Even though you cannot see them, they are definitely there. Who are these unseen onlookers who accompany us every second of our lives, witnessing our words, deeds, and possibly even our thoughts? They are angels.

You may be surprised to know that the Bible contains more than three hundred direct references to angels. What the Bible says about angels is stirring, eye-opening, awe inspiring, comforting, and challenging. It whets our appetite for Heaven, for in Heaven we will be allowed to associate more directly with these marvelous creations called angels than we do down here and now.

**In Heaven we will associate with
amazing creatures called angels.**

Angel Myths

Because there is so much misinformation floating around about angels, it is helpful to examine some of the most common myths. Let's look briefly at several of the legends of angels and compare them with what the Bible clearly teaches.

1. Angels are adorable chubby babies with wings and/or pale females.

Walking into many gift shops, one might imagine that the

primary role of angels is purely decorative. Holiday angels are soft, luscious creatures, all ruffles and fluff. They are sweet, beautiful ladies wearing kind, nonjudgmental smiles. Valentine angels are pink, plump, dimpled, whimsical, cute, baby cupids carrying little bows. Neither representation is anything anyone would take seriously.

The Bible paints a drastically different portrait of angels. Every angel described in the Bible is an awe-inducing adult male. (For examples, see Daniel 10:8; Luke 1:12–13, 30; 2:9–10; Matthew 28:2–5). Repeatedly, when you read of an angel appearing to a human, the first words out of the angel's mouth are "Fear not." Why? Because seeing a real angel would easily scare you out of your wits. Even the fearless man of God, Daniel, described his encounter with an angel this way, "I had no strength, my faced turned deathly pale and I was helpless" (Daniel 10:8). When angels appeared to the shepherds, announcing the birth of Messiah, the Bible says those poor shepherds were terrified. Words like *cute* and *cuddly* don't go with any of the angels described in the Bible.

2. Angels must earn their wings.

The cute concept that angels must earn their wings by doing good deeds comes from the mild angel character "Clarence" in the classic holiday movie *It's a Wonderful Life*. It makes for a great story, but it has no basis in truth. The fact is that such a notion is never mentioned in the Bible. When God created angels, they already had their wings and seem to be able to hide them when they take a human form.

3. Angels lounge in Heaven playing harps.

I think this myth comes from a misunderstanding of Revelation 5. A close reading of that passage makes it clear that the only persons said to be playing harps in Heaven are the twenty-four elders, who are redeemed *humans,* not angels (Revelation 5:8–14).

4. Angels reproduce.

I hate to break it to you, but you cannot marry an angel. Oh, she may be a cute girl, but technically she can't be an angel. Also, note that angels don't make babies. I know the old song says it's angels who create really special people, mixing sunlight and star dust to make a "dream come true." It makes for a nice song, but not a true one. The fact is, Jesus Himself stated clearly that angels do not marry or reproduce (Mark 12:25).

5. Angels are former humans.

A common myth is that when a nice person dies, he or she goes to Heaven and becomes an angel. According to the Bible, humans and angels are two entirely and eternally different classes of beings. We are different species. Humans do not graduate to "angelhood" at death. Instead, we will ultimately receive heavenly *human* bodies similar to the one Jesus had after His resurrection.

Angel Facts

I hope that some of the truths about angel myths did not upset you. If so, don't worry. The rest of the story of angels will enrich and excite you. It will also give you a greater longing for Heaven.

1. Angels are real.

Angels really exist. As we said, there are over three hundred direct references to angels in the Bible. You cannot believe the Bible without believing in angels.

2. Angels are spirit beings.

The writer of the biblical book of Hebrews asks an important rhetorical question when he says, "Are not all angels ministering *spirits* sent to serve those who will inherit salvation?" (Hebrews 1:14, emphasis added). The answer of course is yes, angels are spirits sent to serve us. Humans have a spirit, but we are dominated by our bodies. Angels *are* spirits who can take a bodily form, but most of the time they don't. Therefore, to us they are invisible.

However, in Heaven angels will be visible. We will see them and interact with them. When the apostle John looked into Heaven in the future, he repeatedly saw and spoke with angels (Revelation 5:2; 7:2; 8:3–12; 9:1,13–14; 10:1, 5–9; 11:15; 14:6–9,15–19; 16:2–17; 17:3, 7, 15; 18:1, 21; 19:9, 17; 21:15, 17; 22:1, 6, 8, 16). Hanging out with angels is a major attraction of Heaven.

3. Angels exist to obey God and serve the saved.

Angels are "sent to *serve* those who will inherit salvation" (Hebrews 1:14, emphasis added). David wrote, "Praise the LORD, you his angels, you mighty ones who do his bidding" (Psalm 103:20).

Angels, good and bad, live to obey the will of their superior. Good angels exist to serve those who are born again. If you are a Christian, God's angels exist to aid you. There is no reason to believe that their service will diminish in Heaven. In fact, it will probably be enhanced.

4. Angels were created by God.

God is the only uncreated being in the universe. Angels are not on the same level as God. They are created *by* God (Colossians 1:16; Job 38:4, 7; Psalm 104:4–5). Angels have not always existed. Unlike God, they are not self-existent or self-sufficient.

5. Angels are highly organized in a governmental/military structure.

The Bible speaks of thrones, powers, rulers, and authorities in the current heavenly realm (Colossians 1:16; Ephesians 3:10). Although it is not the focus of this book, we should mention the great unseen war going on in the spirit world right now. Every angel is a part of this war effort. They aren't isolated, wandering souls. They are on-purpose beings whose manner is strictly business. They realize the severity of the spiritual war being waged between God and Satan for your soul. They recognize their position in either the army of light or the army of darkness. They have a tight hierarchy with positions of rank and order.

6. Angels are mighty creatures.

Angels are not cuddly babies or soft ladies. They are called "mighty ones" (Psalm 103:20). One angel had the strength to lift and carry the huge stone in front of Jesus' tomb up the hill (Matthew 28:2). In the future, four angels will have the power to hold back the wind (Revelation 7:1). Later, a single angel will throw into the sea a boulder so large that the wave will drown an entire city (Revelation 18:21). Angels are currently far superior to humans in terms of speed, strength, and intelligence.

7. Angels are immortal.

Jesus says that after the resurrection, humans will be as angels already are, in that we will no longer die (Luke 20:36). You cannot kill an angel. At this time in history, good angels fight with demons in spiritual warfare. Eventually, all evil angels will be imprisoned.

8. *When not taking a humanlike form, angels are described as wind, fire, and stars.*

Angels are spirits. Frequently, the Bible writers describe them in a way we could identify with—flames of fire, bursts of wind, shining stars (Judges 5:20; Job 38:7; Psalm 18:10–14; Hebrews 1:7; Revelation 9:1–2). Even when they do appear in human form, they are bright, shining, brilliantly lit beings.

9. *Angels are only visible when God opens our eyes to see them.*

I love one particular story in 2 Kings. Aram was at war with Israel. The Arameans were mad at God's man, Elisha. Every time they planned an attack, Elisha informed Israel's army as to exactly what the Arameans were going to do. The Arameans got so angry that when they discovered Elisha's location, they sent an entire army to get him. Elisha's servant woke him up in the morning to tell him that the enemy had surrounded the entire town with their army. The servant was terrified, exclaiming, "What'll we do? What'll we do?"

Elisha confidently calmed his consternated servant.

> *"Don't be afraid," the prophet answered.*
> *"Those who are with us are more than those who*
> *are with them." And Elisha prayed, "O LORD,*
> *open his eyes so he may see." Then the LORD*
> *opened the servant's eyes, and he looked and saw*
> *the hills full of horses and chariots of fire all*
> *around Elisha.*
>
> 2 KINGS 6:16–17

God opened the servant's eyes to give him a little glimpse behind the scenes. What did he see? He saw an awesome army of angels surrounding the army of Aram. Elisha prayed and the angels blinded the enemy soldiers. Then Elisha led the enemy army back to his capital. There the king served them lunch and sent them home. Not surprisingly, we never read about them bothering Israel or Elisha ever again.

10. Angels do not compare with Jesus Christ.

The primary point of the book of Hebrews is that Jesus is better than anything else out there. No one or no thing compares to Him, not even angels. He is supreme. Jesus' person and His name are superior to the angels (Hebrews 1:4). Jesus is worthy of worship from angels (1:6). He will sit at the right hand of the Father; they are simply servants (1:8–14). Jesus will ultimately rule the world (2:5).

In Philippians 2 we read that because Jesus left the glories of Heaven to become a man, died on the cross to pay for our sins, and rose from the dead, one day in Heaven every knee will bow and every tongue will confess that He is Lord. It is very clear which knees will bow—*every* knee on earth and in Heaven (Philippians 2:9–11). That means that every knee of every human *and* every knee of every angel will one day bow down and claim Jesus is Lord. He is superior to all, including angels.

11. Angels are not to be worshiped, but were created to lead us to worship God.

Paul warned against the futility of worshiping angels and getting overly caught up in angel sightings (Colossians 2:18). The saddest aspect about the current "angel mania" is that people are choosing angels to be their spiritual touch point, in place of Jesus Christ. People who choke on the hard truths of the Bible and the holiness side of God often substitute angels as a handy compromise of sweet, gooey, nonjudgmental fluff. Yet angels are inadequate spiritual touch points. We all need a genuine relationship with God through the Lord Jesus Christ.

We were created to worship God, not His servants.

Granted, angels are amazing beings. They are smarter, faster, stronger, and more beautiful than any of us. They are so impressive that twice even the apostle John tried to worship them. But, in both cases, the angel said the same thing.

> *At this I fell at his feet to worship him. But he said to me, "Do not do it! I am a fellow servant with you and with your brothers who hold to the testimony of Jesus. Worship God!"*
>
> REVELATION 19:10

> *But he said to me, "Do not do it! I am a fellow servant with you and with your brothers the prophets and of all who keep the words of this book. Worship God!"*
>
> REVELATION 22:9

Worship God!

So What?

In Heaven we will have unparalleled access to and association with awe-inspiring beings called angels. They will do for us then what they desire to do for us now—serve us and help us worship God.

Why not pause right now and worship the One who is superior to the angels? Worship Jesus Christ.

18

Do All Dogs Go
to Heaven?

A young mother was trying to comfort her daughter when her pet kitten died. The mother stroked the little girl's hair and said, "Remember dear, Fluffball is up in Heaven right now with God."

"But Mommy," the little girl sobbed, "what in the world does God want with a dead cat?"

There will be no dead cats in Heaven.

However, the questions often raised are, "Will there be living animals in Heaven? If so, which animals? How do we know?"

Before I answer those questions, consider the following. Someone observed that a dog thinks: "Hey, these people I live with feed me, love me, provide me with a nice warm, dry house, pet me, and take good care of me. . . . They must be gods!" On the other hand, a cat thinks: "Hey, these people I live with feed me, love me, provide me with a nice warm, dry house, pet me, and take good care of me. . . . I must be a god!"

The above facts and my own careful study of the Bible lead me to conclude: There will be animals in Heaven, but probably no cats. (Just kidding about the cats. . .)

We will enjoy animals in Heaven.

Earth has had three heads. Adam was the head of the first Earth. Noah was the head of the Earth cleansed by the flood.

And thirdly, Jesus is coming to be the King of a renewed Earth. God surrounded Adam with *animals* in the Garden of Eden. God instructed Noah to fill a huge boat with *animals* to save them from the flood. When Jesus was born, He was surrounded by *animals* in a barn. God created and loves animals. We should expect God to surround those in Heaven with animals.[1]

Edenizing

Several years ago the concept of Edenizing was introduced to some retirement and long-term nursing facilities. The concept was developed to combat three primary challenges facing seniors in long-term care facilities: loneliness, helplessness, and boredom. The key principle is that the environments need to be seen as habitats for human beings, rather than facilities for the frail and elderly. The major means of making environments more human friendly is providing "close and continuing contact with plants, *animals,* and children, as these relationships offer a pathway to a life worth living." Companion animals (usually dogs, not cats by the way) are introduced to their environments to provide the opportunity to give meaningful care to other living creatures. Proponents claim amazing results.[2]

Edenizing has been successfully proving that people feel more human, and are therefore happier and healthier, when they are around animals, plants, and children. Heaven right now is a restored Garden of Eden, called Paradise. The original Garden of Eden was a festival of plant and animal life. God created *animals* to live in the garden and called them "good" (Genesis 1:20–25). He created man and gave him the primary responsibility for ruling the *animals* (Genesis 1:28). When Adam was created, God surrounded him with animals, so we should expect that there will be animals in Paradise, the restored Garden of Eden.

Noah's Ark

You remember the story. God was brokenhearted by the unrelenting wickedness and corruption of early man, and planned to cleanse the earth (Genesis 6:5–7, 11–13). Noah was the righteous exception, and God decided to spare him and his family (Genesis 6:8–10). God instructed Noah to build a huge boat, or ark, to protect them from the coming flood (Genesis 6:14–17). But that was not all God wanted to spare from destruction. Noah was to fill the huge boat with *animals*, keep them with him, and feed them in order to save them from the flood.

> *You are to bring into the ark two of all living creatures, male and female, to keep them alive with you. Two of every kind of bird, of every kind of animal and of every kind of creature that moves along the ground will come to you to be kept alive. You are to take every kind of food that is to be eaten and store it away as food for you and for them.*
>
> GENESIS 6:19–21

God was so concerned about the animals that He supernaturally sent them to Noah so he could load them onto the ark (Genesis 7:8–9, 15). After the flood subsided, "God remembered Noah *and* all the wild animals and the livestock that were with him in the ark" (Genesis 8:1, emphasis added). God instructed Noah that when he exited the ark, he was to bring all of the animals with him (Genesis 8:17). God promised, "Never again will I destroy all living creatures, as I have done" (Genesis 8:21). God's promise was established in a covenant between God, Noah, *and* the animals.

> *"I now establish my covenant with you and
> with your descendants after you and with every
> living creature that was with you—the birds, the
> livestock and all the wild animals, all those that
> came out of the ark with you—every living crea-
> ture on earth. . . . I will remember my covenant
> between me and you and all living creatures of
> every kind. Never again will the waters become
> a flood to destroy all life. Whenever the rainbow
> appears in the clouds, I will see it and remember
> the everlasting covenant between God and all liv-
> ing creatures of every kind on the earth."*
>
> GENESIS 9:9–10, 15–16

When Noah was spared, God showed how much He valued
animals, and how much He thought man needed animals by
making certain the animals were delivered with him. When He
promised not to destroy Earth again by flood, God was careful to include animals in His covenant. Therefore, we should
expect that God surrounds man with animals in Heaven.

The Peaceable Kingdom of Heaven

Edward Hicks was a Quaker preacher in Bucks County,
Pennsylvania, in the early 1800s. His artistic endeavors provided
modest support for his church activities. In 1833 Hicks created
an American masterpiece entitled "Peaceable Kingdom." In the
work, Hicks gives a pleasant, pastoral portrayal of a lion, tiger,
wolf, bear, and leopard happily lounging with an ox, calf, goat,
and several children. In the background, Quaker statesman
William Penn is seen making peace with the Indians. The painting is a visual sermon based on Isaiah 11:6–9, which describes
peaceful animals coexisting with small children on the renewed
Earth after the coming of Christ.

> *The wolf will live with the lamb, the leopard will lie down with the goat, the calf and the lion and the yearling together; and a little child will lead them. The cow will feed with the bear, their young will lie down together, and the lion will eat straw like the ox. The infant will play near the hole of the cobra, and the young child put his hand into the viper's nest. They will neither harm nor destroy on all my holy mountain, for the earth will be full of the knowledge of the LORD as the waters cover the sea.*

> ISAIAH 11:6–9

Isaiah repeats the Lord's prophecy of peaceful animals on renewed Earth later in his book:

> *"The wolf and the lamb will feed together, and the lion will eat straw like the ox, but dust will be the serpent's food. They will neither harm nor destroy on all my holy mountain," says the LORD.*

> ISAIAH 65:25

From the above two passages we know there will be some, if not all, animals in Heaven. Wolves, lambs, lions, oxen, leopards, calves, yearlings, cows, and even serpents are mentioned.

Horses in Heaven

I love to ride horses. Those big, powerful animals have a strong appeal to humans. When John saw into Heaven, he saw horses. On two separate occasions he saw horses ridden by those in Heaven.

> *I looked, and there before me was a white horse!*
> *. . . Then another horse came out, a fiery red one. . . .*
> *I looked, and there before me was a black horse! . . . I*
> *looked, and there before me was a pale horse!*

> REVELATION 6:2, 4–5, 8

> *I saw heaven standing open and there before*
> *me was a white horse, whose rider is called*
> *Faithful and True. . . . The armies of heaven*
> *were following him, riding on white horses and*
> *dressed in fine linen, white and clean.*

> REVELATION 19:11, 14

Talk to the Animals

Dr. Dolittle is the central character of a series of children's books by British author Hugh Lofting. Dolittle is a doctor who shuns human patients in favor of animals, with whom he can speak in their own languages. He later becomes a naturalist, using his abilities to speak with animals to better understand nature and the history of the world. Dr. Dolittle has become a classic and much-loved character of children's literature. But Dr. Dolittle was not the first to talk to an animal.

Over three thousand years ago, a man named Balaam had an interesting conversation with his donkey. The seemingly "dumb" donkey showed itself to be much wiser than the prophet for hire. Notice the superior intelligence of the animal.

> *Balaam got up in the morning, saddled*
> *his donkey and went with the princes of Moab.*
> *But God was very angry when he went, and the*
> *angel of the LORD stood in the road to oppose*
> *him. Balaam was riding on his donkey, and his*

two servants were with him. When the donkey saw
the angel of the LORD *standing in the road with a*
drawn sword in his hand, she turned off the road
into a field. Balaam beat her to get her back on the
road. Then the angel of the LORD *stood in a nar-*
row path between two vineyards, with walls on both
sides. When the donkey saw the angel of the LORD,
she pressed close to the wall, crushing Balaam's foot
against it. So he beat her again.

NUMBERS 22:21–25

The donkey had greater spiritual insight than Balaam. She could see the angels when he couldn't.

Then the angel of the LORD *moved on ahead*
and stood in a narrow place where there was no
room to turn, either to the right or to the left.
When the donkey saw the angel of the LORD, *she*
lay down under Balaam, and he was angry and
beat her with his staff. Then the LORD *opened the*
donkey's mouth, and she said to Balaam, "What
have I done to you to make you beat me these
three times?"

NUMBERS 22:26–28

God gave the donkey the ability to speak Balaam's language.

Balaam answered the donkey, "You have
made a fool of me! If I had a sword in my hand,
I would kill you right now."
The donkey said to Balaam, "Am I not your
own donkey, which you have always ridden, to

this day? Have I been in the habit of doing this to you?" "No," he said.

NUMBERS 22:29–30

The donkey showed greater reasoning ability than Balaam.

> *Then the LORD opened Balaam's eyes, and he saw the angel of the LORD standing in the road with his sword drawn. So he bowed low and fell facedown. The angel of the LORD asked him, "Why have you beaten your donkey these three times? I have come here to oppose you because your path is a reckless one before me."*

NUMBERS 22:31–32

What does this have to do with Heaven? God gave an animal the ability to talk to a human on Earth, so why shouldn't He also give them the ability to talk to us in Heaven? The serpent could speak in the Garden of Eden (Genesis 3:1–2). Humans are going to get new bodies with enhanced abilities and maybe animals will, as well. If "wild" animals will be changed enough to peacefully coexist with each other and young children (Isaiah 11:6–9), couldn't they be changed enough to speak in our language?

Like all of God's creations, animals were created to praise Him. Praise is a verbal expression of appreciation and adoration. Some feel that animals will verbally join in when we praise God in Heaven.[3]

> *Praise the LORD. . . . Praise the LORD from the earth, you great sea creatures. . . wild animals and all cattle, small creatures and flying birds, kings of the earth and all nations, you princes and all rulers*

on earth, young men and maidens, old men and
children. Let them praise the name of the LORD, *for*
his name alone is exalted; his splendor is above the
earth and the heavens.

PSALM 148:1, 7, 10–13

Then I heard every creature in heaven and on
earth and under the earth and on the sea, and all
that is in them, singing: "To him who sits on the
throne and to the Lamb be praise and honor and
glory and power, for ever and ever!"

REVELATION 5:13

So What?

There will definitely be animals in Heaven. I love my own dog and hope he'll join us in Heaven, though I am not positive that he will. (He does makes a mess in the garbage frequently). But I am confident animals, including dogs, will be there. (Of course, I'm not so sure about cats.)

This knowledge should give those of us who love pets comfort. Knowing that even wild animals will be tamed should give non animal lovers comfort as well. It should also remind us that humans were originally charged with caring for animals. We must be careful how we treat animals, for they may one day tell us off in Heaven.

NOTES

1. Randy Alcorn, *Heaven,* 381.
2. "The Eden Alternative," Data and Resources, http://www.edenalt.com/data/htm#Elm
3. Alcorn, *Heaven,* 378–379.

19

IT'LL BLOW YOUR MIND

"What sort of day was it? A day like all days, filled with those events that alter and illuminate our times. . .and you were there."

When the narrator spoke those words in his deep, dramatic voice, they always captured my attention. For over five seasons, noted broadcaster Walter Cronkite hosted reenactments of historical events in the television series *You Were There*. Shows included "The Landing of the Hindenburg," "The Salem Witchcraft Trials," "The Gettysburg Address," and "The Fall of Troy." The charm of the program was picturing yourself embedded into the most fascinating events of human history.

Unfortunately, the black and white footage, the mediocre acting, and the inexpensive sets did not live up to the promise of the premise. But that will not be the case in Heaven. I believe Heaven will have its own sort of *You Were There* theater that will not only insert you into some of the most amazing events in history, but will also depict the key events in your life. By being there, you will gain a level of understanding otherwise impossible to attain.

When picturing the *You Were There* theater, envision a red brick, 1950s-style theater on a quaint main street in small-town USA. Inside, you smell popcorn in the lobby and hear the seats creak when you sit down.

However, once you sit down and the movie begins, it will be unlike any show you have ever experienced. Miraculously, you will be transported through time and space as an up-close-and-personal unseen spectator of such incredibly amazing events as the creation of the universe, Moses parting the Red Sea, David bringing down Goliath, and Elijah facing down the prophets of Baal. The Bible will no longer be words of black typed on white pages. It will become a living theater, and you will be on stage in every scene you want and need to see.

Imagine being there with Peter, with the spray of the sea in his face, as he walks toward Jesus on the water or tasting the bread Jesus has just broken to feed the five thousand. Picture yourself gasping in awe and then elation when Lazarus walks out of the tomb, newly alive. Listen to the fear in the voices of the disciples just before Jesus walks into the upper room on the night of His resurrection.

You'll feel the heat and hear the voice of God radiating from Moses' burning bush. You'll see the mysterious handwriting on the wall at Belshazzar's party. You'll be stunned with the shepherds as the heavenly host erupts in the sky proclaiming the birth of the Messiah.

I believe you will get to see the role of angels, God's unseen secret agents, played in key proceedings. You will be there with Elisha and his servant when God opens his eyes and he sees the hills full of the angelic army. You will be there when God's angels rout three armies as Jehoshaphat leads his people out in praise and thanks. You'll see Gabriel delivering the prophecy of the seventy weeks to the aged Daniel. You'll see the angels knocking down the walls of Jericho.

Yet, maybe even more importantly, I believe Heaven will give you the opportunity to relive and review the key events of *your* life. You'll have the opportunity to see the joy in Jesus' face as you accepted Him as your Savior. You'll "be there" the first time you tried to share your faith and the Holy Spirit graciously put the right words in your mouth. From a new vantage point, you'll relive those times you fought through bitter tears to a position of resolved faith, and you'll see the Father quietly stroking your hair.

You'll also be there for the crushing, brutal episodes of your life that you never understood before. Now, for the first time, you'll get the rest of the story. You'll receive answers to the gnawing *what, how,* and especially *why* questions in your life. You'll see a clearer, larger, deeper picture. . .and healing, profound healing, will occur.

But enough of what I think or believe we will come to understand once we are in Heaven. Let's look at what we *know* about what we will know in Heaven.

What We Know About What We'll Know in Heaven

> *Now we see but a poor reflection as in a mirror; then we shall see face to face. Now I know in part; then I shall know fully, even as I am fully known.*
>
> 1 CORINTHIANS 13:12

When the apostle Paul wrote the words recorded in the letter to the Corinthians, mirrors were not what they are today. They gave a distorted image. There was a big difference between seeing your face in a mirror and seeing it live, face-to-face. This verse tells us we will see more clearly and understand more fully in Heaven than we can now.

Heaven is a mind-expanding experience.

We Won't Know Everything

We will know much more in Heaven than we do now, but we will not know everything. Only God is infinite; therefore, only God knows everything. We will know more fully, but not exhaustively.

We don't *need* to know everything there is to know. I doubt that I'll *need* to know how many grains of salt are in my salt shaker, or the total number of words ever printed on every book, typewriter, and computer screen in history, or even the batting average of Mickey Mantle in 1961. (It's .317, by the way.)

There are also many things I don't think I will ever *want* to know. I don't wish to know how many earthworms have ever lived. I have no desire to know the intricate details of the life of maggots. There are many things I just don't want to know.

We'll Know Much More Than We Know Now

While it is true we won't know everything in Heaven, we will know much more, much more fully, and much more accurately than we do now. One scholar writes,

> *1 Corinthians 13:12. . .rightly translated, simply says that we will know in a fuller or more intensive way, "even as we have been known, that is without error or misconceptions in our knowledge."*[1]

Many life issues that have always been murky will become crystal clear in the golden light of Heaven. Pieces of the puzzle will come together. Confusing matters will make sense.

We Will Continue to Learn in Heaven

Learning and growing are what keep life from becoming mundane. Contrary to popular opinion, life in Heaven will be anything but mundane. One reason Heaven will be such a vibrant place is because we will continue to learn in Heaven. We will have the time and opportunity to be taught more than we could even imagine on Earth.

Among other things, we will know more about God, the Bible, the mystery of salvation, the complexities of the universe, the history of the world, and more about ourselves than we could possibly know now. In Heaven our capacity for knowing and understanding will be greatly expanded. Also, our opportunity for knowing and understanding will be wildly enhanced. We will have the greatest guides imaginable.

Guided Tours

Growing up, my favorite family vacation was a week spent crawling through the caves of Carter Caves State Park in beautiful Kentucky. My dad, brother, and I spelunked with a fascinating guide named John. John knew the major facts, the offbeat details, and the tantalizing legends. He had a way of sharing them that was absolutely riveting and delightful. His love for the caves was contagious.

Years later, my dad and I took my boys back through the caves, hoping they would enjoy it as much as we had. They didn't and neither did we. Why? John had moved on. Our guides were dry, bland, busy sorts who seemed rather businesslike and bored by it all.

Maybe you have never been much of a fan of science, archaeology, astronomy, biology, botany, ecology, entomology, geology, hydrology, meteorology, or zoology. I think you will be in Heaven, simply because you will be given a guided tour by some of the greatest guides and most amazing scientists who ever lived. But even better, you will have access to the One who made it all! Imagine having an eternity to study the vast complexity of creation at the feet of the Creator!

Great Books

In Heaven we will have time and opportunity to read the greatest books ever written. We know that these books will be there:

1. The Bible (Matthew 24:35; Psalm 119:89). Just think, we can discuss the books at length with each of the thirty-nine or so human writers.

2. The scroll of remembrance, recounting times of fellowship shared by those who feared the Lord (Malachi 3:16). It's possible to have your name written in that book repeatedly.

3. The books containing documentation of every single deed done by every person of all time (Revelation 20:12). Noble deeds, seemingly unnoticed by history, will be recorded for all who look in the books.

4. The book of life, containing information about every one of God's people (Revelation 3:5; 13:8; 17:8; 20:12, 15; 21:27). Your name and mine can be in that book.

5. A record of David's tears (Psalm 56:8). I would guess the tears of others may also be written there, as God has also saved "the prayers of the saints" (Revelation 5:8).

Beyond these heavenly books, there will probably be no shortage of other outstanding reading material. With some of the greatest authors in history having unlimited time and expanded intellect, we can imagine they will author some truly incredible books while they are in Heaven. In Heaven you will have the time to read the book you never had time for and write that book you have always wanted to write.

Adult Education

In Heaven we will have the opportunity to learn skills that we did not have the time or ability to acquire on earth. I hope to draw and paint the pictures I have mentally recorded during my lifetime. I also anticipate painting heavenly sights that can only be imagined on Earth. I hope to learn to play the piano and the guitar really well. I want to understand the nuances of music well enough to write a symphony. I want to write songs. Why not? I will have access to wonderful teachers and all of eternity to practice.

We'll Know and Understand Ourselves Better Than We Do Now

In Heaven we will not only have more information, we'll have a better context for that information. We'll see facts through the 20/20 vision of eternity. We'll see the events of life as they are reflected in the eyes of the Master, especially the events of our lives.

The point of Mitch Albom's best-selling fictional story *The Five People You Meet in Heaven* is that the first five people you meet in Heaven will illuminate the unseen or misunderstood connections of our earthly lives.

> *"People think of heaven as a paradise garden,*
> *a place where they float on clouds and laze in*
> *rivers and mountains. But scenery without solace*
> *is meaningless. This is the greatest gift God can*

give you: to understand what happened in your
life. To have it explained. It is the peace you have
been searching for."2

While I don't fully accept Albom's view of Heaven, I do think he is right about one thing. From the vantage point of Heaven, we will accurately be able to understand our lives and the meaning of the events of our lives. We will finally have answers to the "why?" questions that taint our joy and plague our minds down here on Earth. Missing pieces of the puzzle will be supplied.

So What?

Don't be frustrated by all you can't and don't understand now. In Heaven you will be continually learning and growing as a person. The day is coming when you will know and understand much more than you ever imagined possible. All of the various events of your life will finally make sense.

NOTES

1. Wayne Gruden, *Systematic Theology: An Introduction to Biblical Doctrine* (Grand Rapids: Zondervan, 1994), endnote on 1162.
2. Mitch Albom, *The Five People You Meet In Heaven* (Hyperion, NY: 2003), 35

WHERE DREAMS COME TRUE

20

"De plane! De plane!"

So began the wildly popular early 1980s television show *Fantasy Island*. Each week two guests came to Fantasy Island to have their fantasy fulfilled. Their mysterious host, the suave, white-suited Mr. Roarke, would sometimes do the impossible in order to grant their wishes. Somehow, the magical island could accommodate every dream, even if it meant visiting another time period, meeting a special person, or getting William Shakespeare to write a play. But there was always a twist to the fulfillment of the fantasy, giving the guests greater insight into themselves. The one constant from week to week was that at the sight of incoming visitors, Mr. Roarke's midget assistant, Tattoo, would scurry up to the bell tower, ring the bell, and shout, "De plane! De plane!"

Fantasy Island was a mediocre television show, but a very appealing idea. Wouldn't you love to go someplace where dreams come true? You can.

The Real Fantasy Island

The last several months, as I have pored over all that the Bible said about Heaven and eternity, I have discovered dozens of tremendous truths about Heaven. Some of my favorites include learning that Mom and Dad are having a splendid time in Paradise, the best parties in the universe are held in Heaven, and

Heaven is anything but boring. I also look forward to enjoying my awesome new body, hanging out with angels, and having pets, maybe even all the perpetual puppies I want. I am especially thrilled to know that I might be able to fly. I am deeply challenged to prepare for Heaven now by living for eternity. Most important, I am eager to see God face to face in Heaven. But if I had to sum Heaven up with one epitaph, it might be this:

Heaven is the place where dreams come true.

God Is the Giver of Dreams

The story of the Bible is the story of God planting big dreams deep in human hearts. God gave a childless pagan, Abram (meaning "exalted father"), the calling of being the father of nations and changed his name to Abra*ham* (meaning "father of many," Genesis 12:1–2). God gave a boy named Joseph the dream of becoming a great leader (Genesis 37:5–10). Moses was given the desire to deliver his people (Exodus 2:11–12). Hannah's longing was for motherhood (1 Samuel 1:11).

We all have a dream or dreams etched deep into our DNA. On Earth, most never recognize their dreams. Many fewer ever see their fantasies fulfilled. Some scheme and sweat to chase a dream. Others deny their unfulfilled desires, hoping the dull ache will go away. But it never really goes away, does it?

God Is the Fulfiller of Dreams

We know the names of Abraham, Joseph, Moses, and Hannah because their dreams came true. Abraham saw his fantasy of fatherhood fulfilled as he fathered two entire nations of people—the Hebrews and the Arabs (Genesis 12:1–3, 6–7; 16:1–12; 17:20–21, 26). Joseph was promoted to a position in charge of one of the strongest nations on Earth (Genesis

41:39–41). Moses led God's people out of four hundred years of bondage (Exodus 12:33–42). Hannah got pregnant, delivered a son, and dedicated him to the Lord. Her son, Samuel, ended up leading a nation back to God (1 Samuel 2:19–20, 24–28; 3:19–21). No doubt, God is the fulfiller of dreams.

David, whose dream of becoming king was gloriously fulfilled, wrote a verse that acknowledges God to be the giver and fulfiller of dreams. "Delight yourself in the LORD, and he will give you the desires of your heart" (Psalm 37:4).

God Is the Rewarder of Faith

Hebrews 11 is one of the greatest chapters in the Bible. It could be called "The Faith Chapter," "The Hall of Faith," or my favorite, "Heaven's Heroes." In the first thirty-four verses, we see joyous examples of God's faithful people being rewarded on Earth for their faith. He tells of the rewarded faith of Enoch, Noah, Abraham, Moses' parents, and Moses himself. The writer builds a great crescendo of testimony to the power of faith.

> *By an act of faith, Israel walked through the Red Sea on dry ground. The Egyptians tried it and drowned. By faith, the Israelites marched around the walls of Jericho for seven days, and the walls fell flat. . . .*
>
> *I could go on and on, but I've run out of time. There are so many more—Gideon, Barak, Samson, Jephthah, David, Samuel, the prophets. . . .Through acts of faith, they toppled kingdoms, made justice work, took the promises for themselves. They were protected from lions, fires, and sword thrusts, turned disadvantage to advantage,*

> *won battles, routed alien armies. Women received*
> *their loved ones back from the dead.*
>
> HEBREWS 11:29–30, 32–35 THE MESSAGE

Did you catch that? God did not "just kinda, sorta" reward their faith. He did major-league miracles. Walking through the Red Sea on dry ground and watching the massive walls of Jericho falling down flat were major miracles. God indeed rewards faith. Hebrews said faithful people conquered kingdoms, shut the mouth of lions, routed foreign armies, even saw their dead raised to life again! Wow, it truly can't get any better than that.

But then the mood of Hebrews 11 suddenly darkens.

> *Others were tortured and refused to be*
> *released, so that they might gain a better resur-*
> *rection. Some faced jeers and flogging, while still*
> *others were chained and put in prison. They were*
> *stoned; they were sawed in two; they were put to*
> *death by the sword. They went about in sheep-*
> *skins and goatskins, destitute, persecuted and mis-*
> *treated—the world was not worthy of them. They*
> *wandered in deserts and mountains, and in caves*
> *and holes in the ground. These were all com-*
> *mended for their faith, yet none of them received*
> *what had been promised.*
>
> HEBREWS 11:35–39

What happened? Being tortured, flogged, chained and put in prison, stoned, and sawn in two is no health, wealth, and happiness reward for faith. Neither is being destitute, persecuted, and mistreated. Trusting in God did not cause these good people to reach their destinies on Earth. In fact, just the opposite occurred—faith led to horrible results. None of these people ever saw the fulfillment of their faith. Their dreams were not reached on Earth. Their faith was unrewarded. Why? God had planned something better (Hebrews 11:40). In other words, Earth is not the end of the line or the final chapter. Rewards will come in Heaven. Earth has no reward big enough for this type of faith (Hebrews 11:38).

How do we deal with the disappointments of unfulfilled fantasies, unrewarded faith, and unattained dreams? We remember that Heaven is the only place where some dreams come true.

Misplaced Priorities

Occasionally, in the place where I exercise, the television is on. One day the show that was being broadcast was about an incredibly attractive and talented family that had left behind most of their Christian roots and integrity to intently pursue big-time fame and fortune in Hollywood. Beating the odds, they quickly succeeded in reaching their dreams of world-renowned celebrity status.

As I watched the story of their lives, I felt a profound sense of sadness. They had systematically sold out in order to reach earthly dreams. One gave away her reputation, another sacrificed her virginity, a third walked away from his ministry. . .all to reach shallow, temporal dreams. They left God behind to chase dreams which, when viewed through the lens of Heaven, will be nothing more than a tiny blip on the radar screen of eternity. They had given up so much in order to gain what they will one day understand to be so very little.

I wonder how often I have been guilty of also chasing my self-centered, earthly dreams. How often have I found the profound sting of disappointment when they are unfulfilled or worse, the hollow emptiness when they are?

True Dream Catchers

One of the rich privileges of Heaven will be meeting people who, while on Earth, made incredible sacrifices for the gospel. They certainly weren't wealthy on Earth. They were not famous. No one down here even remembers their names. Pain, persecution, suffering, sorrow, misery, and, for some, martyrdom described their lives.

Don't feel sorry for them. They weren't pursuing earthly dreams. They had eternity in view all along. In Heaven they will be incredibly rewarded.

> *"I tell you the truth," Jesus replied, "no one
> who has left home or brothers or sisters or mother or
> father or children or fields for me and the gospel will
> fail to receive a hundred times as much in this pres-
> ent age (homes, brothers, sisters, mothers, children
> and fields—and with them, persecutions) and in the
> age to come, eternal life."*
>
> MARK 10:29–30

So What?

Maybe living for God has caused you to put some of your dreams on hold. Maybe there are deep desires and ardent longings that cannot, or will not, ever be fulfilled on Earth. Your unfulfilled dream involves holding a child or having a true friendship. It could involve taking a trip or attaining a level of accomplishment. Take hope. In Heaven there will be time and opportunity to reach for dreams unimagined on Earth. Friends, don't ever forget: If your dreams are from God, Heaven—not Earth—is the place where real dreams come true.

21

You Can Get There from Here

My friend Dave Watson is the pastor of a fine church on Staten Island in New York City. Recently, he sent me a video his church had produced entitled, "How to Get to Heaven from New York City." The video had some music, a few testimonies, and a brief talk by Pastor Dave.

In his talk, Dave told the wonderful story of how God sent His Son Jesus to Earth to die for our sins. He said that by trusting Jesus as Savior, a person would not only have a life wonderfully changed now, but would also have a place reserved in Heaven. Then he gave watchers the opportunity to pray a prayer expressing their faith in Jesus Christ.

As I viewed the video, I was reminded that the way to get to Heaven is the same from any place. However, all roads won't get you there. Jesus is the only way.

Many Ways to the Post Office?

Years ago I spent a summer doing street evangelism in England. I was on a team of young people who shared Jesus in schools, prisons, churches, and on street corners. During our street meetings, we usually sang several songs to draw a crowd. Then one of us would briefly tell the audience how much Jesus loved them. Our American accents never failed to get and keep their attention.

We would share how Jesus lived a sinless life, yet undeservedly died in our place as a sacrifice for our sin. We told how He rose from the dead to prove that He was God, and that God was satisfied with His payment for our sin. After a prayer, we would spread out through the crowd and try to engage them in conversation. Then we would discuss their response to the message of Jesus' death and resurrection for their sins.

Often near the beginning of the conversations we would ask them, "If you died today are you sure that you would go to Heaven?" This simple question usually gave us the opportunity to share how Jesus had changed our lives and why we had confidence that we were on our way to Heaven.

One day a nicely dressed gentleman who looked to be somewhere in his early sixties gave me a very condescending smile. "Young man," he said, "I am happy that your religion gives you such bold confidence about your eternal destiny. But I believe that Jesus is just one of many ways to Heaven. Every religion and philosophy is just a different way to the same place."

When I gave him a frown, he continued, "You see, right now we are sitting in a park. The post office is on the other side of town. From here there is more than one way to the post office. In the same way, there is more than one way to Heaven."

I looked at him and said, "But sir, we aren't talking about getting to the post office, we are talking about something infinitely more important—getting to Heaven."

He frowned as I continued. "Jesus claimed to be the only way to Heaven. In John 14:6 He emphatically said, 'I am the way and the truth and the life. No one comes to the Father except through me.'

"So, sir, you have to decide if Jesus was a liar, or a lunatic, or if He really is the Lord God. If there are many ways to Heaven and Jesus knew there were other ways, then He was a liar, and not a good man like you say. Following Him wouldn't be one of the ways to Heaven. Sir, do you really think Jesus was a liar?"

He shook his head no.

I continued, "If there truly are many ways to Heaven and Jesus sincerely believed that He is the only way, then He must have been a lunatic. Certainly trusting in a lunatic would never get anyone to Heaven. Sir, do you really believe that Jesus was a lunatic? Do you think I am a nut for following Him?"

Again he slowly shook his head no.

"Then your only other option is that He knew exactly what He was saying and what it meant. He really is *the way*, the truth, and the life. No one does go to the Father in Heaven *except through Him*. Jesus really was the Son of God. He did live a sinless life. He did die for our sins and He rose from the dead. He is the Lord of life. No one else did all of that for you, no one else could. But Jesus did because He loves you. He is the way to get to Heaven."

He rose to leave. "Son, you have given me much to think about. I will definitely read your pamphlet tonight."

"Where are you going?" I asked.

Sheepishly he said, "You are not going to believe this, but I've got to go to the post office."

How to Get to Heaven from Anywhere on Planet Earth
No matter where you live, the route to Heaven is the same for everyone. Whether you live in Russia, China, or West Virginia, there is one way that will get you to Heaven—faith in Jesus Christ.

Salvation is a faith process leading to an event. This process consists of several necessary steps. Maybe you have heard people speak of being "saved." Let me show you the seven biblical steps of faith that a person takes to be saved. A person needs to believe the following facts:

1. There is a God.
The Bible assumes the existence of God. It starts with these words, "In the beginning God. . ." (Genesis 1:1). His creation verifies His reality.

> *For since the creation of the world God's*
> *invisible qualities—his eternal power and divine*
> *nature—have been clearly seen, being understood*
> *from what has been made, so that men are with-*
> *out excuse.*

ROMANS 1:20

Do you believe there is a God? If so, you have enough faith to go to step 2.

2. I am responsible to God.

The Bible says, "So then, each of us will give an account of himself to God" (Romans 14:12). It also says, "Just as man is destined to die once, and after that to face judgment" (Hebrews 9:27). One day each of us must stand before God and give an account of our lives to Him.

Do you accept the fact that you are accountable to God? If so, go to step 3.

3. I have failed my responsibility; I have not lived up to God's standard; I have broken God's laws. In other words, I have sinned.

It is as though God demands that our lives hit the bull's-eye on the target of moral righteousness before we can enter Heaven. Some of us may get closer than others, but all of us have missed the bull's-eye, because we are not perfect. Failing to hit this bull's-eye is sin. The Bible says, "All have sinned and fall short of the glory of God" (Romans 3:23). There are no perfect people. The Bible is quite clear, "There is no one righteous, not even one" (Romans 3:10). It also says, "If we claim to be without sin, we deceive ourselves and the truth is not in us" (1 John 1:8).

Have you perfectly kept all of the Ten Commandments? (See

Exodus 20.) Can you even name all ten? Do you deem it to be true that you have sinned by failing to perfectly keep God's commands? If so, go to step 4.

4. My sin has alienated/separated me from my God.

Every sin we commit is like a brick in a wall of separation between us and God, because He is holy. The Bible says, "Your iniquities [sins] have separated you from your God" (Isaiah 59:2).

This separation from God, when carried to its logical conclusion, leads to death. The Bible says, "For the wages of sin is death" (Romans 6:23). Sin has the awful price tag of death. Death, as used in the Bible, speaks of separation. Physical death is the separation of the soul from the body when you stop breathing. Spiritual death is the separation of the soul from God. Eternal death is the separation of the soul from God, forever. The Bible says that we deserve death on all three levels because we have sinned against God.

Do you believe this? If so, go to step 5.

5. Jesus never sinned.

Jesus, the Son of God, was like mankind in every way except one. He never sinned. His sinless nature is seen throughout the Bible. For example, the Bible says He "has been tempted in every way, just as we are—yet *was without sin*" (Hebrews 4:15, emphasis added). By being sinless, He alone could take away our sin. As John wrote, "But you know that he appeared so that he might take away our sins. And *in Him is no sin*" (1 John 3:5, emphasis added).

It is as though God has an accounting book in Heaven. On the first page is the ugly record of all our sins and the fact that they add up to death and separation from God. But on the second page is the sinless record of Jesus Christ. So, instead of deserving death, He deserved life and union with God.

GOD'S ACCOUNTING BOOK

BAD NEWS	GOOD NEWS
US	JESUS
+SIN	-SIN
DEATH	LIFE
Page 1	Page 2

Do you believe that Jesus, the Son of God, never sinned? If so, go to step 6.

6. I can only be reconciled to God through Jesus Christ.

The third page of God's accounting book has the sad news that Jesus died on the cross two thousand years ago for our sins. He died in our place. He took our penalty. He did this in order to pay for our sins and to bring us to God.

That is why Jesus is the only way to God. Everyone human has sinned. None of us are perfect. Only Jesus Christ is the sinless Son of God, capable of paying for all of our sins.

If we place our faith in Him, and only Him, we can receive the gift of eternal life in Heaven. Read these verses carefully:

> *God made him who had no sin to be sin for us, so that in him we might become the righteousness of God.*
>
> 2 CORINTHIANS 5:21

> *For Christ died for sins once for all, the righteous for the unrighteous, to bring you to God.*
>
> 1 PETER 3:18

*The wages of sin is death, but the gift of God is
eternal life in Christ Jesus our Lord.*

ROMANS 6:23

*For it is by grace you have been saved,
through faith—and this not from yourselves, it is
the gift of God—not by works, so that no one can
boast.*

EPHESIANS 2:8–9

SAD NEWS	GLAD NEWS
JESUS	US
+OUR SIN	+FAITH IN JESUS
DEATH IN OUR PLACE	ETERNAL LIFE
Page 3	Page 4

Do you believe that Jesus died to pay for all of your sins? Do you believe eternal life is a free gift to be received by faith in Christ? If so, go to step 7. You have enough faith to be saved and to go to Heaven.

7. I am willing to receive the gift of eternal life.

Are you willing to be saved from your sin and receive God's free gift of eternal life? Receiving the gift of eternal life is an act of simple faith. It is as simple as ABC: **A**dmit you need to be saved. **B**elieve completely on Christ as the only one who can save you. **C**all upon Him to take control of your life and save you.

God promises, "Everyone who calls on the name of the Lord will be saved" (Romans 10:13). You can do that right now. If that is your desire, read this prayer and pray it to God as you do.

> *Dear God,*
>
> *I admit that I am not perfect. I have sinned. Please forgive me.*
>
> *I do not deserve eternal life. I have come short of Your standard of righteousness. I admit I need a Savior.*
>
> *I believe that Jesus took my place and died for my sin. I believe that He rose from the dead to prove He can offer eternal life.*
>
> *Now I call upon You to be my Lord and Savior. I personally commit myself completely to You.*

So What?

Congratulations! If you have sincerely expressed your faith in the Lord Jesus as your Savior by calling out to Him through this prayer, the Bible says that you are saved (Romans 10:13). I will look you up when we all get to Heaven.

FINAL THOUGHTS

22

Q: How long is eternity?
A: Eternity is a very *long* time.

John Ankerberg illustrates eternity by comparing it to the efforts of a parakeet to pick up a single grain of sand in its beak, fly to the moon, drop it off, and return to Earth. If each round trip took a million years, and you commanded him to transport all the sand from all the beaches and deserts on Earth until there was no more sand, all the millions of years it took him to accomplish the task would just begin eternity. Eternity is a very long time.[1]

Where we spend eternity will be determined by whether or not we have trusted Jesus Christ as our Savior. Knowing this motivates us to be certain that we've been born into God's forever family through faith in Jesus Christ. I pray that reading this book did not merely give you good information about Heaven, but more importantly provided you with firm resolution to make certain you will be there by faith in Jesus.

How we spend eternity will be determined by how we live on Earth today. Our ability and capacity to enjoy and experience all that will be Heaven is established by how we live on Earth. Knowing this should motivate us to live for God now. I pray that reading this book has fueled an unrelenting passion to go all out for God in every area of your life, every day of your life, no matter what. You will never regret it.

Eternity is long. Live for God.

The author of Hebrews used this truth to motivate his readers who were suffering persecution.

> *Remember those earlier days after you had*
> *received the light, when you stood your ground in*
> *a great contest in the face of suffering. Sometimes*
> *you were publicly exposed to insult and persecu-*
> *tion; at other times you stood side by side with those*
> *who were so treated. You sympathized with those in*
> *prison and joyfully accepted the confiscation of your*
> *property, because you knew that you yourselves had*
> *better and lasting possessions. So do not throw away*
> *your confidence; it will be richly rewarded.*

HEBREWS 10:32–35

NOTES

1 John Ankerberg, "How Long Is Eternity?" Ankerberg Theological Research Institute, http://www.ankerberg.org/Articles/practical-christianity/PC0101W1. htm (May 15, 2006)